ROAD ATLAS

HANDY BRITAIN
& IRELAND

CONTENTS

II Key to road map symbols

III Distance table

IV Counties map

1 Key to map pages

2 Road maps of Great Britain at 8 miles to 1 inch

58 Road maps of Ireland at 19 miles to 1 inch

62 Index to road maps of Ireland

64 Index to road maps of Great Britain

www.philips-maps.co.uk

First published in 2010 by Philip's
a division of Octopus Publishing Group Ltd
www.octopusbooks.co.uk
Carmelite House, 50 Victoria Embankment
London EC4Y 0DZ
An Hachette UK Company
www.hachette.co.uk

Fifth edition 2021, first impression 2021
ISBN 978-1-84907-577-0

Cartography by Philip's, copyright © 2021 Philip's

Road map symbols

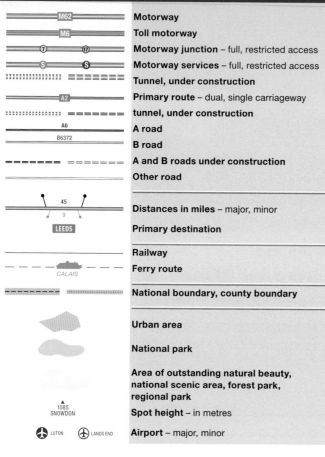

	Motorway
	Toll motorway
	Motorway junction – full, restricted access
	Motorway services – full, restricted access
	Tunnel, under construction
	Primary route – dual, single carriageway
	tunnel, under construction
	A road
	B road
	A and B roads under construction
	Other road
	Distances in miles – major, minor
	Primary destination
	Railway
	Ferry route
	National boundary, county boundary
	Urban area
	National park
	Area of outstanding natural beauty, national scenic area, forest park, regional park
	Spot height – in metres
	Airport – major, minor

Scales

Pages 2–56
1:506880, 1cm = 5.07 km, 1 in = 8 miles

```
0    5    10    15    20    25    30km
```

```
0         5          10         15        20 miles
```

Pages 58–61
1:1200000, 1cm = 12km, 1 in = 18.94 miles

```
0    10    20    30    40    50km
```

```
0         10         20        30 miles
```

Abbreviated local authority areas

BCP	Bournemouth, Christchurch and Poole	8H
BD	Bridgend	13G1
BF	Bracknell Forest	16J
BG	Blaenau Gwent	13E1
BL	Blackpool	26B
BN	Blackburn with Darwen	27C
CB	City and County of Bristol	14J
CBH	City of Brighton and Hove	10J
CE	City of Edinburgh	40F
CF	Cardiff	7C1
CM	Clackmannanshire	40D
CN	City of Nottingham	22A
CY	Caerphilly	7B1
DD	Dundee City	51P
DE	Derby City	22B
DN	Darlington	32C
ED	East Dunbartonshire	39C11
ER	East Renfrewshire	39E9
FK	Falkirk	39C13
GC	Glasgow City	39D10
HL	Hartlepool	32A6
HN	Halton	26G6
IC	Inverclyde	39D8
KH	Kingston upon Hull	29A9
LE	Leicester City	22E5
LU	Luton	16C5
MB	Middlesbrough	32C6
MR	Merthyr Tydfil	13E14
NEL	North East Lincolnshire	29D11
NL	North Lanarkshire	39D13
NP	Newport	7C12
NPT	Neath Port Talbot	13F11
PL	Plymouth	3F12
PM	Portsmouth	9G11
RC	Redcar and Cleveland	33C8
RD	Reading	16H2
RF	Renfrewshire	39D9
RT	Rhondda Cynon Taff	7B9
SD	Southend-on-Sea	17G14
SL	Slough	16G4
SN	Stockton-on-Tees	32B6
SO	Southampton	9F9
ST	Stoke-on-Trent	21A9
SW	Swindon	15G10
TB	Torbay	4G2
TF	Torfaen	7A11
TK	Thurrock	17G12
TW	Telford and Wrekin	20E7
WA	Warrington	26G7
WD	West Dunbartonshire	39C9
WK	Wokingham	16J2
WL	West Lothian	40F3
WM	Windsor and Maidenhead	16H3

Distance table

How to use this table

Distances are shown in miles and, in light type, in kilometres. For example, the distance between Birmingham and Dover is **194** miles or 312 kilometres.

```
London
517
332 Aberdeen

211 445
340 716 Aberystwyth

117 420 114
188 676 183 Birmingham

107 564 207 147
172 908 333 237 Bournemouth

52 573 253 163 92
84 922 407 262 148 Brighton

122 493 125 81 82 147
196 793 201 130 132 237 Bristol

54 471 214 100 154 116 169
87 758 344 161 248 187 272 Cambridge

157 505 105 103 117 182 45 190
253 813 169 166 188 293 72 306 Cardiff

301 221 224 196 343 370 277 264 289
484 356 360 315 552 596 446 425 465 Carlisle

71 588 297 (194) 174 82 202 125 238 389
114 947 478 312 280 132 325 201 383 626 Dover

448 67 376 349 495 517 430 406 441 152 523
721 108 605 562 797 832 692 654 710 245 842 Dundee

390 125 320 292 439 456 373 345 385 96 462 56
628 201 515 470 707 734 600 555 620 154 744 90 Edinburgh

260 504 56 170 222 291 154 270 112 297 331 460 399
418 811 90 274 357 468 248 435 180 478 533 740 642 Fishguard

510 149 430 392 539 575 486 479 485 206 596 127 144 486
821 240 692 631 867 926 782 771 781 332 959 204 232 782 Fort William

397 145 320 292 439 468 373 372 385 96 488 83 44 376 101
639 233 515 470 707 753 600 599 620 154 786 134 71 605 163 Glasgow

109 468 102 56 99 159 35 123 56 247 191 410 349 153 454 346
175 753 164 90 159 256 56 198 90 398 307 660 562 246 731 557 Gloucester

76 535 281 167 187 128 217 67 246 336 125 469 413 337 543 432 196
122 861 452 269 301 206 349 108 396 541 201 755 665 542 874 695 316 Harwich

269 439 111 148 288 334 206 270 216 231 360 394 330 191 349
433 707 179 238 463 538 332 435 348 372 580 634 536 269 705 531 307 562 Holyhead

550 105 486 458 597 617 509 549 262 622 132 158 542 66 166 504 569 474
885 169 782 737 961 993 867 813 884 422 1001 212 254 872 106 267 811 916 763 Inverness

663 232 601 574 724 741 668 630 680 391 746 259 285 671 195 295 628 693 603 129
1067 373 967 924 1165 1193 1075 1014 1094 629 1201 417 459 1080 314 475 1011 1116 970 208 John o' Groats

184 364 223 134 264 245 233 139 244 158 256 295 234 280 365 224 169 196 231 394 518
296 586 359 216 425 394 375 224 393 254 412 475 377 451 594 409 272 316 372 634 834 Kingston upon Hull

297 692 313 281 205 308 200 374 245 477 381 642 574 353 686 573 235 390 405 741 868 421
478 1114 504 452 330 496 322 602 394 768 613 1033 924 568 1104 922 378 628 652 1193 1397 678 Land's End

189 327 169 113 255 260 194 145 232 119 260 258 202 237 329 215 174 223 176 360 487 55 405
304 526 272 182 410 419 312 233 373 192 418 415 325 381 530 346 280 359 283 579 784 89 652 Leeds

131 383 199 90 209 197 183 85 208 191 202 314 258 272 399 291 159 155 216 427 554 44 371 68
211 616 320 145 336 317 295 137 335 307 325 505 415 438 642 468 256 249 347 687 892 71 597 109 Lincoln

202 341 104 93 234 272 161 194 169 120 299 286 216 160 209 216 140 265 102 382 511 130 361 75 129
325 549 167 150 377 438 259 312 272 193 481 460 348 257 530 348 225 427 164 615 822 209 581 121 208 Liverpool

185 340 129 80 227 257 161 165 183 119 276 285 215 197 329 215 126 228 124 373 500 95 361 40 84 35
298 547 208 129 365 414 259 266 295 192 444 459 346 317 530 346 203 367 200 600 805 153 581 64 135 56 Manchester

286 235 257 207 347 352 299 241 325 57 358 166 110 329 253 146 266 308 272 268 395 132 498 92 159 168 132
460 378 414 333 558 567 481 388 523 92 576 267 177 529 407 238 428 496 438 431 636 212 802 148 256 270 212 Newcastle upon Tyne

114 496 276 166 214 175 252 62 262 289 174 422 366 344 282 406 100 422 465 280 679 589 552 811 620 328 117 501
183 798 444 267 344 282 406 100 422 465 280 679 589 552 811 620 328 117 501 852 1053 240 678 283 169 354 298 425 Norwich

57 483 154 64 90 108 74 83 108 260 141 433 372 205 472 356 52 145 238 532 656 192 274 168 137 172 144 260 145
92 777 248 103 145 174 119 134 174 418 227 697 599 330 760 573 84 233 383 856 1056 309 441 270 221 277 232 418 233 Oxford

218 615 237 203 128 224 122 293 167 399 300 642 595 495 157 309 328 664 790 355 89 316 293 283 320 ... 199
351 990 382 327 206 361 196 472 269 642 483 888 798 425 958 797 253 497 528 1069 1271 571 143 509 472 455 455 660 552 320 Plymouth

159 360 159 76 216 226 161 120 194 152 245 291 235 215 348 248 126 187 168 393 520 65 361 33 46 72 38 125 146 135 283
256 579 256 122 348 364 259 193 312 245 394 468 378 346 560 399 203 301 270 632 837 105 581 53 74 116 61 201 235 217 455 Sheffield

77 547 201 128 31 61 76 148 121 324 143 500 428 253 541 433 105 164 293 598 723 256 128 214 206 64 159 155 199
124 880 323 206 50 98 122 238 195 521 230 805 705 375 871 697 169 264 472 963 1164 412 367 373 328 385 356 521 332 103 243 320 Southampton

402 228 325 297 444 475 378 379 390 101 496 167 124 392 195 84 343 410 338 262 379 259 585 220 298 221 220 158 403 379 500 263 445
647 367 523 478 715 765 608 610 627 163 798 268 200 631 314 135 552 660 544 421 610 417 942 354 480 356 354 649 610 805 153 716 Stranraer

194 507 73 119 167 222 85 227 41 309 274 473 412 412 496 409 267 184 572 696 264 285 248 235 195 187 347 301 141 206 217 161 417
312 816 117 192 269 357 137 365 66 497 441 761 663 108 798 658 143 430 296 921 1120 425 459 399 375 314 301 559 485 227 332 349 259 671 Swansea

207 319 195 130 269 275 222 165 244 121 282 250 194 261 330 271 189 228 204 352 479 37 411 24 75 99 64 84 181 181 333 52 258 222 272
333 513 314 209 443 443 357 266 393 195 454 402 312 420 531 349 304 367 328 566 771 60 661 39 121 159 103 135 291 291 536 84 415 357 438 York
```

Map labels: John o' Groats, Inverness, Aberdeen, Fort William, Dundee, Glasgow, Edinburgh, Stranraer, Newcastle upon Tyne, Carlisle, Leeds, York, Kingston upon Hull, Manchester, Lincoln, Holyhead, Liverpool, Sheffield, Norwich, Birmingham, Aberystwyth, Cambridge, Gloucester, Fishguard, Oxford, Harwich, Swansea, Cardiff, Bristol, London, Southampton, Bournemouth, Brighton, Dover, Plymouth, Land's End

Counties and unitary authorities

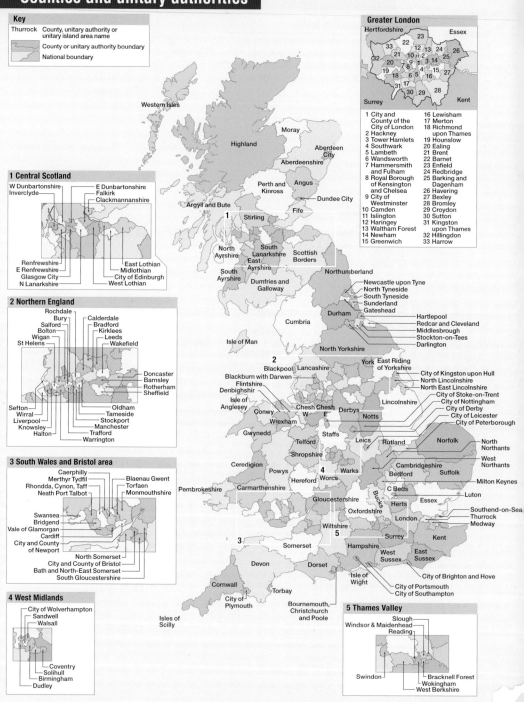

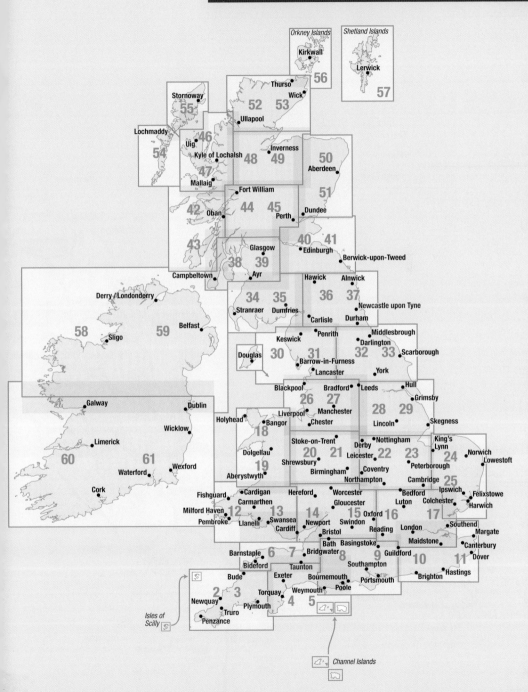

1

Orkney Islands
Kirkwall
56

Shetland Islands
Lerwick
57

Thurso
Wick
Stornoway
55
52
53
Ullapool
Lochmaddy
46
54
Uig
Kyle of Lochalsh
48
49
Inverness
50
Aberdeen
47
Mallaig
Fort William
51
42
44
45
Dundee
Oban
Perth
43
40
41
Glasgow
Edinburgh
38
39
Berwick-upon-Tweed
Campbeltown
Ayr
Hawick
Alnwick
Derry / Londonderry
34
35
36
37
Stranraer
Dumfries
Newcastle upon Tyne
Carlisle
Durham
58
59
Belfast
Middlesbrough
Sligo
Keswick
Penrith
Darlington
Douglas
30
31
32
33
Scarborough
Barrow-in-Furness
Lancaster
York
Galway
Dublin
Blackpool
Bradford
Leeds
Hull
Wicklow
26
27
Grimsby
Liverpool
Manchester
28
29
Holyhead
Bangor
Chester
Lincoln
Skegness
Limerick
18
Stoke-on-Trent
Nottingham
King's
60
61
Wexford
Dolgellau
20
21
Derby
22
23
Lynn
24
Norwich
Waterford
19
Shrewsbury
Leicester
Peterborough
Lowestoft
Aberystwyth
Birmingham
Coventry
Cambridge
25
Cork
Northampton
Ipswich
Felixstowe
Fishguard
Cardigan
Hereford
Worcester
Bedford
Colchester
Harwich
Milford Haven
Carmarthen
12
13
14
Gloucester
15
Luton
16
17
Pembroke
Llanelli
Swansea
Newport
Oxford
London
Southend
Cardiff
Bristol
Swindon
Reading
Margate
Barnstaple
Bath
Basingstoke
Guildford
Maidstone
Canterbury
6
7
Bridgwater
8
9
10
11
Dover
Bideford
Taunton
Southampton
Brighton
Hastings
Bude
Exeter
Bournemouth
Portsmouth
2
3
Torquay
Weymouth
Poole
Newquay
4
5
Truro
Plymouth
Isles of
Scilly
Penzance

Channel Islands

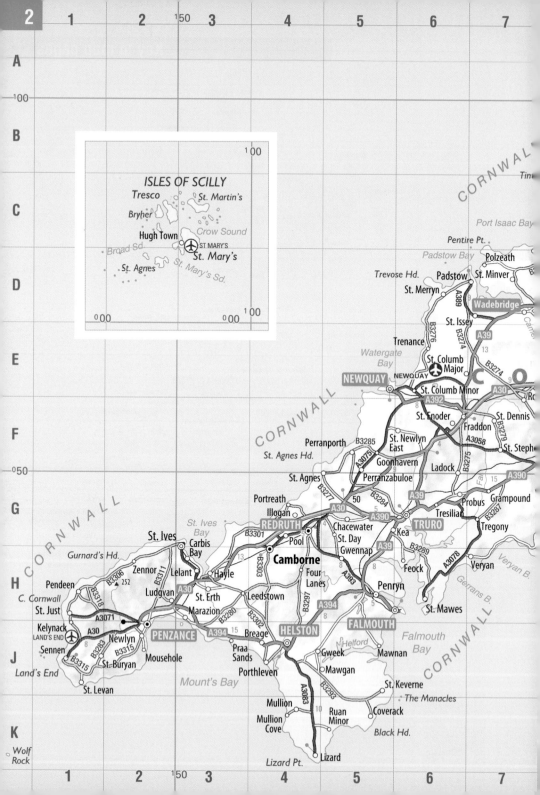

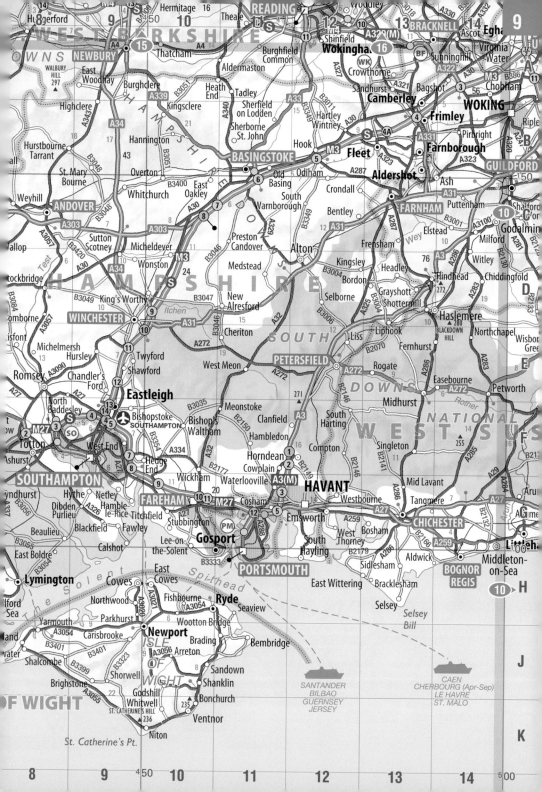

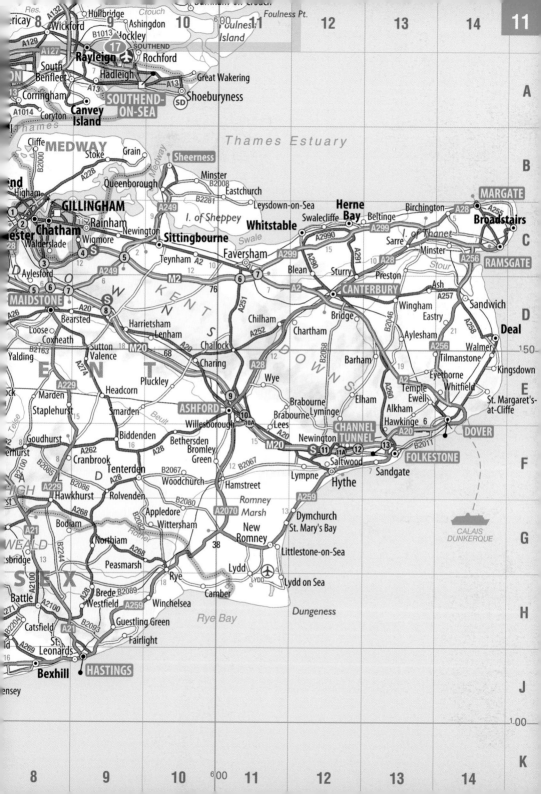

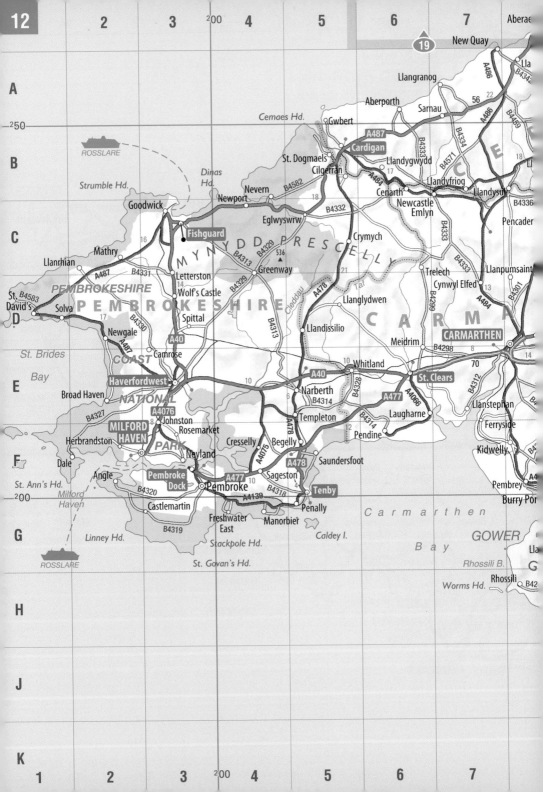

WARWICKSHIRE

Feckenham · Astwood Bank · Alcester · Barford · Harbury · Daventry
Inkberrow · Weedon Bec
Wellesbourne · 71
Upton Snodsbury · Bidford-on-Avon · **STRATFORD-UPON-AVON** · Gaydon · Fenny Compton · Byfield
Salford Priors · Kineton
Harvington · Cleeve Prior · Ettington · EDGE HILL · Wardington · Middleton Cheney
EVESHAM · Bretforton · Halford · 226 · Wroxton · **BANBURY** · King's Sutton · Brackley
Eckington · Mickleton · Shipston-on-Stour · B4035 · Aynho
Ashton under Hill · ILMINGTON DOWNS 260 · Swalcliffe · Bloxham
BREDON HILL 293 · Chipping Campden · Long Compton · Deddington · Ardley
Ashchurch · Broadway · Blockley · Moreton-in-Marsh · Hook Norton · Middle Barton · Upper Heyford · **Bicester**
Bishop's Cleeve · Stanway · **Chipping Norton** · Enstone · Kirtlington · Ambrosden
Winchcombe · CLEEVE CLOUD 330 · Stow-on-the-Wold · Churchill · Charlbury · Woodstock · Bletchingdon · Islip
Prestbury · **CHELTENHAM** · Bourton-on-the-Water · Shipton under Wychwood · Witney · Kidlington · Stanton St. John
Charlton Kings · Andoversford · Northleach · Burford · Yarnton · **OXFORD**
Withington · Aldsworth · Brize Norton · Eynsham TOLL · Botley · Wheatley
North Cerney · Bibury · Carterton · Stanton Harcourt · Cumnor · Kennington
Stratton · Fairford · Bampton · Standlake · Kingston Bagpuize · Sandleigh · Radley · Stadh...
CIRENCESTER · Lechlade-on-Thames · Buckland · **Abingdon-on-Thames**
South Cerney · Highworth · Faringdon · Dorchester · Sutton Courtenay · Benson · Walling...
Kemble · Watchfield · Grove · Harwell · Didcot · Blewbury · Cholsey
Ashton Keynes · Cricklade · Shrivenham · Uffington · Wantage · Woodco...
Minety · Purton · Stratton St. Margaret · Ashbury · WHITE HORSE HILL 261 · Farnborough · East Ilsley · Streatley
Charlton · **SWINDON** · Wanborough · Lambourn · Compton · Pangbourne
Great Somerford · Royal Wootton Bassett · Wroughton · Chiseldon · Aldbourne · Great Shefford · Hampstead Norreys · Theale
Brinkworth · Lyneham · Ogbourne St. George · Welford · Hermitage
Hilmarton · Broad Hinton · Whitonditch · Hungerford · **NEWBURY**
CHIPPENHAM · Calne · Cherhill · Avebury · **Marlborough** · Froxfield · **WEST BERKSHIRE** · Thatcham
Lacock · Beckhampton · TAN HILL 294 · WALBURY HILL 297 · East Woodhay · Burghclere
Bromham · WANSDYKE · Vale of Pewsey · A346 · Pewsey · Burbage · Tadl...
Melksham · Devizes

COTSWOLDS · **WORCESTERSHIRE** · **OXFORD** HILLS · **BERKSHIRE DOWNS** · **WESSEX** · **NORTH WESSEX** · **MARLBOROUGH DOWNS**

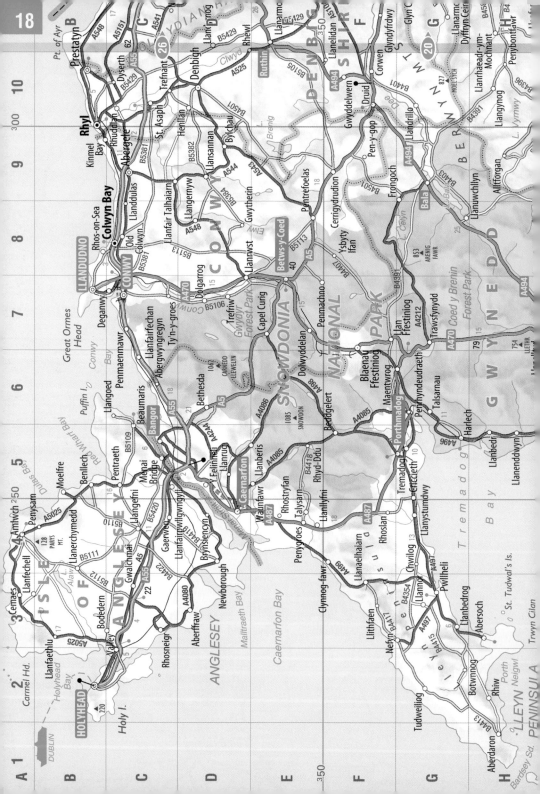

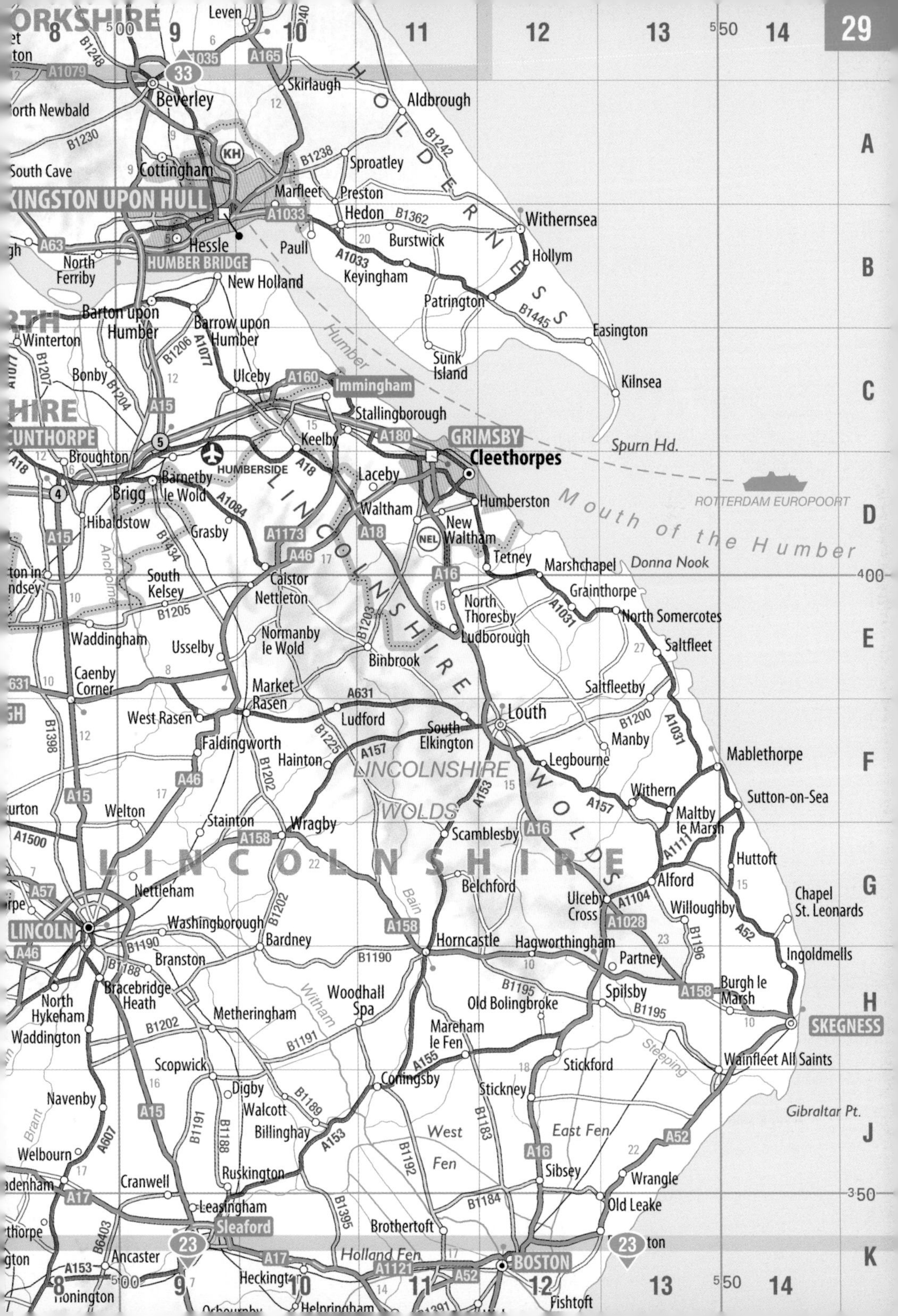

YORKSHIRE

8 9 10 11 12 13 14

Leven
Skirlaugh
Beverley
Cottingham
Aldbrough
Sproatley
KINGSTON UPON HULL
Marfleet Preston Hedon
Hessle Paul Burstwick Withernsea
HUMBER BRIDGE Keyingham Hollym
North Ferriby New Holland Patrington
Barton upon Humber Barrow upon Humber Sunk Island Easington
Winterton Ulceby Kilnsea
Bonby A160 Immingham
SCUNTHORPE Stallingborough Spurn Hd.
Broughton Keelby GRIMSBY Cleethorpes
Barnetby le Wold Laceby Humberston
Brigg HUMBERSIDE Waltham New Waltham Mouth of the Humber
Hibaldstow Grasby Tetney Marshchapel Donna Nook
Waddingham Calstor North Thoresby Grainthorpe ROTTERDAM EUROPOORT
South Kelsey Nettleton Normanby le Wold Ludborough North Somercotes
Usselby Binbrook Saltfleet
Caenby Corner Market Rasen Saltfleetby
West Rasen Ludford Louth Manby Mablethorpe
Faldingworth Hainton South Elkington Legbourne Sutton-on-Sea
LINCOLNSHIRE WOLDS Withern Maltby le Marsh
Welton Stainton Wragby Scamblesby Huttoft
Nettleham Belchford Ulceby Cross Alford Willoughby Chapel St. Leonards
LINCOLN Washingborough Bardney Horncastle Hagworthingham Partney Ingoldmells
Branston Old Bolingbroke Spilsby Burgh le Marsh
North Hykeham Bracebridge Heath Metheringham Woodhall Spa Mareham le Fen SKEGNESS
Waddington Scopwick Coningsby Stickford Wainfleet All Saints
Navenby Digby Walcott Stickney Gibraltar Pt.
Welbourn Billinghay West Fen East Fen
Cranwell Ruskington Sibsey Wrangle
Leasingham Brothertoft Old Leake
Sleaford Holland Fen
Ancaster Heckington BOSTON
Honington Fishtoft

ISLE OF MAN

Isle of Whithorn

Maryport
Fothergill
Flimby
Seaton
WORKINGTON
Great Clifton
Harrington
Distington
Parton
WHITEHAVEN
Frizington
St. Bee's Hd.
Cleator Moor
St. Bees
Egremont
Beckermet
Calder Bridge
Sellafield
Gosforth
Seascale
Drigg
Ravenglass

Crosby
Bothel
Dearham
Cockermout
Thornth
Bassenthwa
Grummock Water
Ennerdale Water
Bu
LA
DIST
Wast Water
NATI
PA
Bootle
BLACK COMBE
600
Whicham
Haverigg
Dalton-in-Fu
BARROW-IN-FURNESS
Vickerstown
I. of Walney
Hilpsford

Pt. of Ayre
Cranstal
Andreas
Bride
Sulby
Ramsey
Ballaugh
Maughold
Kirk Michael
Maughold Hd.
SNAEFELL 620
Ramsey Bay
Peel
Laxey
St. John's
Glenmaye
Onchan
Foxdale
SOUTH BARRULE 483
Douglas
Bradda Hd.
Colby
Ballasalla
Port Erin
Port St. Mary
Castletown
ISLE OF MAN
Langness
Calf of Man

HEYSHAM
BELFAST (April-Sept)
DUBLIN (April-Sept)
LIVERPOOL

	8	9	10	11	5'00	12	13	14

A

REDCAR
Marske-by-the-Sea
Saltburn-by-the-Sea **B**
Skelton Brotton
A174
Loftus Staithes
A173 RC 23
Guisborough Kettle Ness
B1366 A174 Hinderwell
A171 20 Lythe **C**
51 **WHITBY**
Castleton Egton Sneaton
Esk Sleights Hawsker **D**
Goathland Robin Hood's Bay
454 Fylingdales
RTH YORK MOORS Moor Staintondale 5'00
NATIONAL PARK A169 19
Rosedale Cloughton **E**
Hodge Abbey Burniston
Dove 20 A171
Hutton-le-Hole Lockton Scalby
Kirkbymoorside A170 **SCARBOROUGH**
aulx Seven Ayton A165 **F**
Helmsley Thornton-le- Eastfield
27 Pickering Dale 16 Ebberston A170 Seamer B1261
Vale of Pickering Snainton A64 Filey
B1258 17
Hovingham Rye Sherburn Staxton **G**
The Carrs B1249 Hunmanby Filey Bay
B1257 21 Burton
HOWARDIAN Malton A64 Rillington Weaverthorpe Fleming B1229 Flamborough
Terrington Norton B1253 B1255 Flamborough
lington I R E Hd. **H**
Sheriff B1248 Rudston
Hutton Langtoft B1253
Strensall Acklam Sledmere B1249 Kilham A614 Burton Bridlington
Fridaythorpe Garton-on- 13 Agnes Bay
Haxby A64 A166 the-Wolds Nafferton
New Earswick Wetwang Lissett **J**
YORK A166 Driffield Beeford Skipsea
A1079 Stamford W O L D S 46 B1242
Dunnington Bridge **EAST RIDING** North 16
CITY OF A1079 19 B1246 Bainton Hutton Frodingham Hornsea
YORK B1228 A164 **OF** Cranswick B1249 A165 B1244
A19 Elvington Barmby **YORKSHIRE** Leven B1240 4'50
Wheldrake Moor Pocklington A614 Middleton on
Escrick 16 Hayton the Wolds A1035
28 Ilme-on- Market 29 augh
Spalding-moor Weighton A1079 everley Aldbrough **K**

| | 8 | | 10 | | 11 | 5'00 | 12 | 13 | 14 |

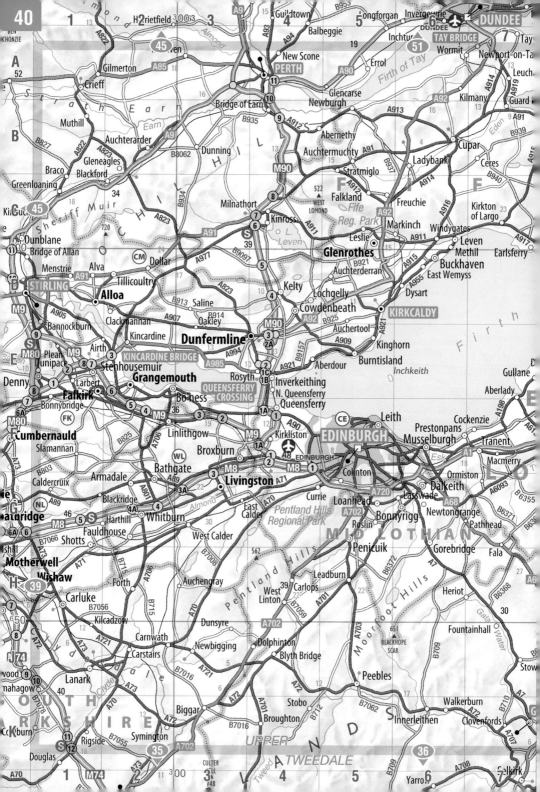

A

51
Inchcape Rock

St. Andrews

Kingsbarns

Dunino
B9131
A917
B940
Fife Ness

B9171
Crail
Kilrenny
Anstruther
Pittenweem
St. Monance
lie
I. of May
7·00

D

of Forth

Bass Rock
North Berwick
eton
B1347
A198
Whitekirk
A S T
Dunbar
Barns Ness
A1
East Linton
58
Haddington
Spott 23
B6370
Garvald
Cockburnspath
B6369
H I A N
Ecclaw
St. Abb's Head
Gifford
Lammermuir Hills
Grantshouse
A1
A1107
St. Abb's

535
MEIKLE
SAYS LAW
A6112
Coldingham
Eyemouth
B6355
Reston
L A M M
Ayton
Burnmouth
B6353
Longformacus
B6438
Preston
Chirnside
16
Whiteadder Water
Duns
Foulden
A6105
BERWICK-UPON-TWEED

Westruther
B6456
A6105
Whitsome
B6461
Tweedmouth
6·50
Polwarth
B6460
Tweed
Norham
Scremerston
Lauder
A697
21
Greenlaw
Swinton
A698
13
A1
B6364
M E R S E
A6089
Gordon
A6112
Ancroft
B6354
Goswick
Holy I.
A6105
9
A68
Leitholm
Barmoor Castle
Earlston
B6397
A6089
Stichill
Coldstream
A698
Lowick
Ross
Budle Bay
ALASHIELS
B6356
Smailholm
Crookham Flodden
B6353
30
Bamburgh
B6360
Kelso
B6396
B6352
13
B6525
Belford
A6091
36
Maxwellheugh
Doddington
37
B6349
Seahouses
Melrose
B6404
A697
Lucker
Newtown
Roxburgh
B6351
Kirknewton
A697
00
Chathill
Boswells
9
A699
10
B6352
Town
11
12
13
14
B1340

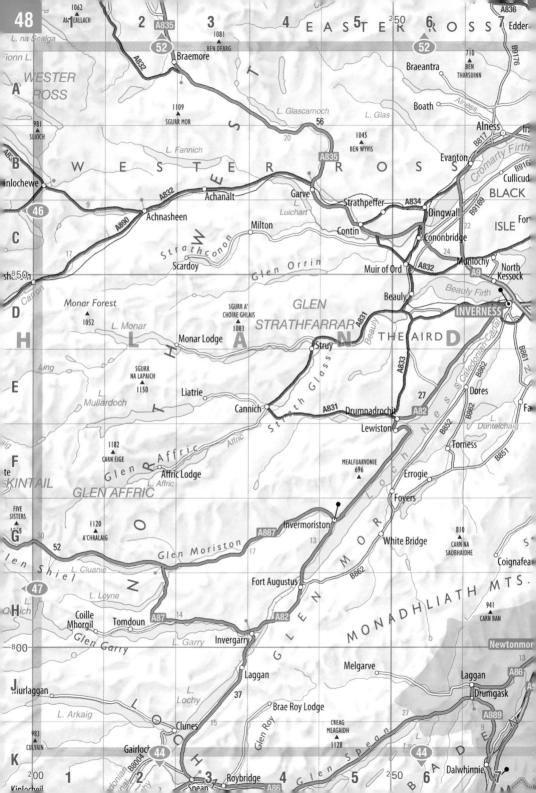

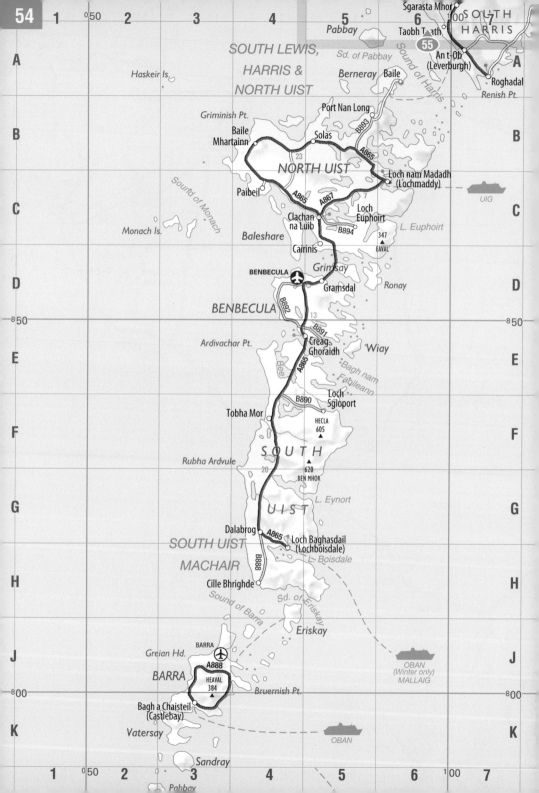

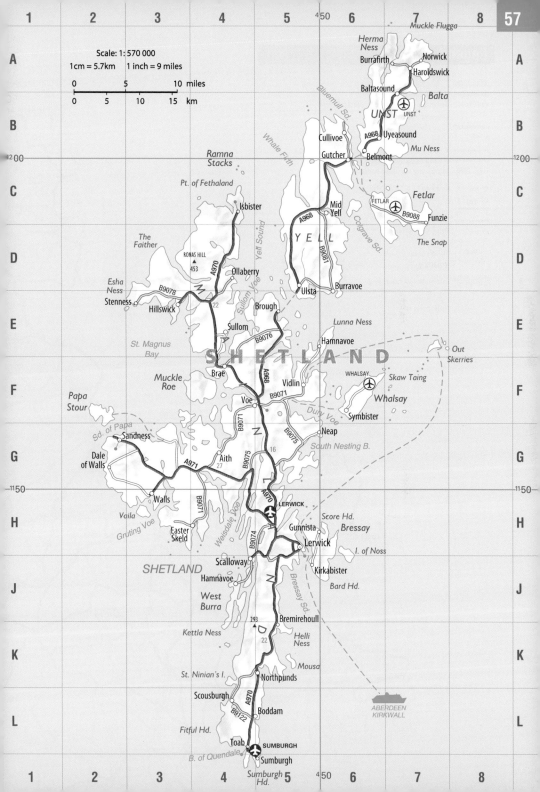

Scale: 1:570 000

1cm = 5.7km   1 inch = 9 miles

0 ... 5 ... 10 miles

0 ... 5 ... 10 ... 15 km

Muckle Flugga

Herma
Ness

Burrafirth ... Norwick
Haroldswick
Baltasound
Balta

UNST

A968 ... Uyeasound

Cullivoe ... Mu Ness

Gutcher ... Belmont

Ramna
Stacks

Pt. of Fethaland

Bluemull Sd.

Whale Firth

FETLAR ... Fetlar

B9088 ... Funzie

The Snap

Isbister

The
Faither

Mid
Yell

YELL

A968

B9081

Colgrave Sd.

RONAS HILL
▲
453

Ollaberry

A970

Yell Sound

Ulsta ... Burravoe

Esha
Ness

B9078

M

22

Stenness

Hillswick

Sullom Voe

Brough

Lunna Ness

Out
Skerries

St. Magnus
Bay

Sullom

B9076

Hamnavoe

S H E T L A N D

Muckle
Roe

Brae

A968

Vidlin

WHALSAY

Skaw Taing

Papa
Stour

Voe

N

B9071

Whalsay

Sd. of Papa

Symbister

Sandness

B9075

16

Neap

Dale
of Walls

Aith

27

Dury Voe

South Nesting B.

A971

A970

Walls

B9071

B9075

L

LERWICK

Score Hd. ... Bressay

Vaila

Gruting Voe

Weisdale Voe

B9074

Gunnista

Lerwick

I. of Noss

Easter
Skeld

Scalloway

A

Kirkabister

Bard Hd.

SHETLAND

Hamnavoe

West
Burra

N

Bremirehoull

Bressay Sd.

293
▲
22

Kettla Ness

Helli
Ness

Mousa

D

St. Ninian's I.

Northpunds

A970

Scousburgh

Boddam

ABERDEEN
KIRKWALL

B9122

Fitful Hd.

Toab ... SUMBURGH

B. of Quendale ... Sumburgh

Sumburgh
Hd.

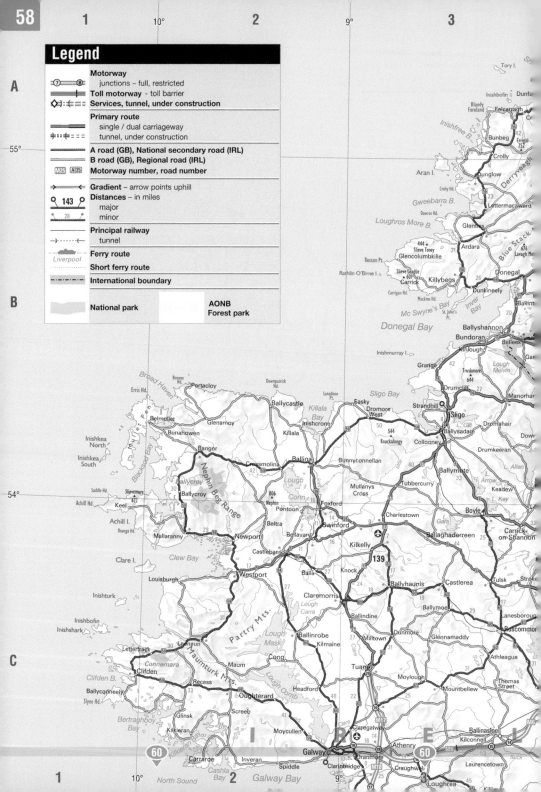

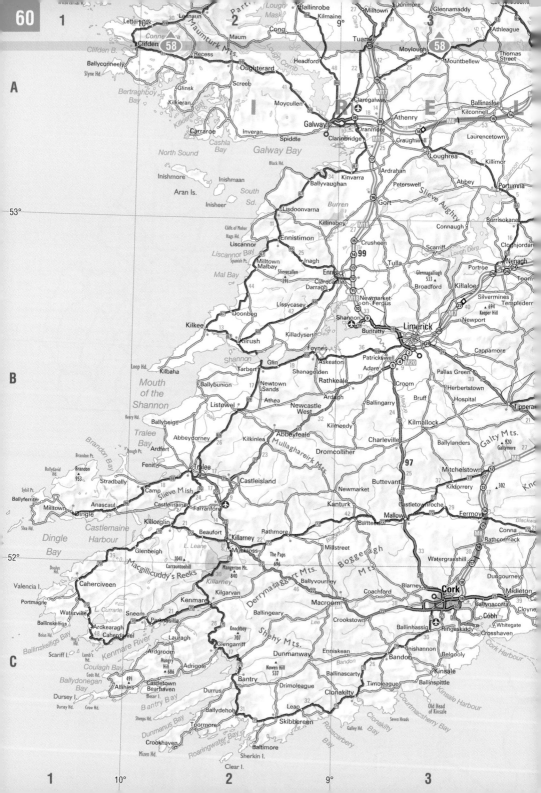

Index to road maps of Ireland

A

Abbey 60 A3
Abbeydorney 60 B2
Abbeyfeale 60 B2
Abbeyleix 61 B4
Adare 60 B3
Adrigole 60 C2
Aghalee 59 B5
Ahoghill 59 B5
Allihies 60 C1
Anascaul 60 B1
Annalong 59 B6
Annestown 61 B4
Antrim 59 B5
Ardagh 60 B2
Ardara 58 B3
Ardee 59 C5
Ardfert 60 B2
Ardglass 59 B6
Ardgroom 60 C2
Ardkearagh 60 C1
Arklow 61 B5
Armagh 59 B5
Armoy 59 A5
Arthurstown 61 B5
Ashbourne 59 C5
Askeaton 60 B3
Athboy 59 C5
Athea 60 B2
Athenry 60 A3
Athleague 58 C3
Athlone 61 A4
Athy 61 B5
Augher 59 B4
Aughnacloy 59 B5
Aughrim 61 B5

B

Bailieborough 59 C5
Balbriggan 59 C5
Balla 58 C2
Ballaghaderreen 58 C3
Ballina 58 B2
Ballinalack 59 C4
Ballinamore 59 B4
Ballinascarty 60 C3
Ballinasloe 60 A3
Ballindine 58 C3
Ballingarry
Limerick 60 B3
Tipperary 61 B4
Ballingeary 60 C2
Ballinhassig 60 C3
Ballinrobe 58 C2
Ballinskellings 60 C1
Ballinspittle 60 C3
Ballintra 58 B3
Ballivor 59 C5
Ballon 61 B5
Ballybay 59 B5
Ballybofey 59 B4
Ballybunion 60 B2
Ballycanew 61 B5
Ballycarry 59 B6
Ballycastle
Antrim 59 A5
Mayo 58 B2
Ballyclare 59 B6
Ballyconneely 58 C1
Ballycotton 60 C3
Ballycroy 58 B2
Ballydehob 60 C2
Ballyferriter 60 B1
Ballygawley 59 B4
Ballygowan 59 B6
Ballyhaunis 58 C3
Ballyheige 60 B2
Ballyjamesduff 59 C4
Ballylanders 60 B3
Ballylynan 61 B4
Ballymahon 59 C4
Ballymena 59 B5
Ballymoe 58 C3
Ballymoney 59 A5
Ballymore 59 C4
Ballymote 58 B3
Ballynacorra 60 C3
Ballynagore 61 A4
Ballynahinch 59 B6
Ballynure 59 B6
Ballyragget 61 B4
Ballysadare 58 B3
Ballyshannon 58 B3
Ballyvaughan 60 A2
Ballyvourney 60 C2
Ballywalter 59 B6
Baltimore 60 C2
Baltinglass 61 B5
Banbridge 59 B5
Bandon 60 C3
Bangor
Down 59 B6
Mayo 58 B2
Banteer 60 B3
Bantry 60 C2
Beaufort 60 B2
Belcoo 59 B4
Belfast 59 B6
Belgooly 60 C3
Bellananagh 59 C4
Bellavary 58 C2
Belleek 58 B3
Belmullet 58 B2
Beltra 58 C2
Belturbet 59 B4
Beragh 59 B4
Birr 61 A4
Blackwater 61 B5
Blarney 60 C3
Blessington 61 A5
Borris 61 B5
Borris-in-Ossory 61 B4
Borrisokane 60 B3
Borrisoleigh 61 B4
Boyle 58 C3
Bracklin 59 C5
Bray 61 A5
Broadford 60 B3
Broughshane 59 B5
Bruff 60 B3
Bunahowen 58 B2
Bunbeg 58 A3
Bunclody 61 B5
Buncrana 59 A4
Bundoran 58 B3
Bunmahon 61 B4
Bunnyconnellan 58 B2
Bunratty 60 B3
Bushmills 59 A5
Butler's Bridge 59 B4
Buttevant 60 B3

C

Caher 61 B4
Caherciveen 60 C1
Caherdaniel 60 C1
Caledon 59 B5
Callan 61 B4
Camp 60 B2
Cappamore 60 B3
Cappoquin 61 B4
Carlingford 59 B5
Carlow 61 B5
Carndonagh 59 A4
Carnew 61 B5
Carnlough 59 B6
Carraroe 60 A2
Carrick 58 B3
Carrickart 59 A4
Carrickfergus 59 B6
Carrickmacross 59 C5
Carrick-on-Shannon 58 C3
Carrick-on-Suir 61 B4
Carrigallen 59 C4
Carryduff 59 B6
Cashel 61 B4
Castlebar 58 C2
Castlebellingham 59 C5
Castleblaney 59 B5
Castlebridge 61 B5
Castlecomer 61 B4
Castlederg 59 B4
Castledermot 61 B5
Castleisland 60 B2
Castlemaine 60 B2
Castlemartyr 60 C3
Castlepollard 59 C4
Castlerea 58 C3
Castletown Bearhaven 60 C2
Castletownroche 60 B3
Castlewellan 59 B6
Cavan 59 C4
Celbridge 61 A5
Charlestown 58 C3
Charleville 60 B3
Clarecastle 60 B3
Claregalway 60 A3
Claremorris 58 C3
Clarinbridge 60 A3
Clashmore 61 B4
Claudy 59 B4
Clifden 58 C1
Clogh 61 B4
Cloghan
Donegal 59 B4
Offaly 61 A4
Clogheen 61 B4
Clogher 59 B4
Cloghjordan 60 B3
Clonakilty 60 C3
Clonaslee 61 A4
Clondalkin 61 A5
Clones 59 B4
Clonmany 59 A4
Clonmel 61 B4
Clonmellon 59 C4
Clonord 59 C4
Clonroche 61 B5
Cloone 59 C4
Clough 59 B6
Cloyne 60 C3
Coachford 60 C3
Coagh 59 B5
Coalisland 59 B5
Cóbh 60 C3
Coleraine 59 A5
Collon 59 C5
Collooney 58 B3
Comber 59 B6
Cong 58 C2
Conna 60 B3
Connaugh 60 B3
Cookstown 59 B5
Coolgreany 61 B5
Cooneen 59 B4
Cootehill 59 B4
Cork 60 C3
Craughwell 60 A3
Creeslough 59 A4
Creeve 59 B5
Crolly 58 A3
Crookhaven 60 C2
Crookstown 60 C3
Croom 60 B3
Crossakiel 59 C4
Crosshaven 60 C3
Crossmolina 58 B2
Crumlin 59 B5
Crusheen 60 B3
Cullaville 59 B5
Cushendall 59 A5

D

Daingean 61 A4
Dalkey 61 A5
Darragh 60 B2
Delvin 59 C4
Derrygonnelly 59 B4
Derrylin 59 B4
Derry/Londonderry 59 B4
Dervock 59 A5
Dingle 60 B1
Donaghadee 59 B6
Donegal 58 B3
Doonbeg 60 B2
Downhill 59 A5
Downpatrick 59 B6
Dowra 58 B3
Draperstown 59 B5
Drimoleague 60 C2
Drogheda 59 C5
Dromahair 58 B3
Dromcolliher 60 B3
Dromore
Down 59 B5
Tyrone 59 B4
Dromore West 58 B3
Drumcliff 58 B3
Drumkeeran 58 B3
Drumquin 59 B4
Drumshanbo 58 B3
Drumsna 59 C4
Dublin 61 A5
Duleek 59 C5
Dunboyne 59 C5
Dundalk 59 B5
Dundrum 59 B6
Dunfanaghy 59 A4
Dungannon 59 B5
Dungarvan 61 B4
Dungiven 59 B5
Dunglow 58 B3
Dungourney 60 C3
Dunkineely 58 B3
Dun Laoghaire 61 A5
Dunlavin 61 A5
Dunleer 59 C5
Dunloy 59 A5
Dunmanway 60 C2
Dunmore 58 C3
Dunmore East 61 B5
Dunmurry 59 B5
Dunshaughlin 59 C5
Durrow 61 B4
Durrus 60 C2

E

Easky 58 B3
Edenderry 61 A4
Edgeworthstown 59 C4
Eglinton 59 A4
Emyvale 59 B5
Enfield 59 C5
Ennis 60 B3
Enniscorthy 61 B5
Enniskean 60 C3
Enniskillen 59 B4
Ennistimon 60 B2

F

Falcarragh 58 A3
Farranfore 60 B2
Feeny 59 B4
Fenagh 59 B4
Fenit 60 B2
Ferbane 61 A4
Fermoy 60 B3
Ferns 61 B5
Fethard
Tipperary 61 B4
Wexford 61 B5
Finnea 59 C4
Fintona 59 B4
Fivemiletown 59 B4
Fontstown 61 A5
Foxford 58 C2
Foynes 60 B2
Freshford 61 B4

G

Galway 60 A2
Garrison 58 B3
Garvagh 59 B5
Gilford 59 B5
Glenamoy 58 B2
Glenarm 59 B6
Glenavy 59 B5
Glenbeigh 60 B2
Glencolumbkille 58 B3
Glendalough 61 A5
Glenealy 61 B5
Glengarriff 60 C2
Glennamaddy 58 C3
Glenties 58 B3
Glin 60 B2
Glinsk 60 A2
Gorey 61 B5
Gort 60 A3
Gortin 59 B4

Gowran 61 B4
Graiguenamanagh . . 61 B5
Granard 59 C4
Grange 58 B3
Greencastle 59 A5
Greenisland 59 B6
Greystones 61 A5

H

Hacketstown 61 B5
Headford 58 C2
Herbertstown 60 B3
Hillsborough 59 B5
Holycross 61 B4
Holywood 59 B6
Hospital 60 B3

I

Inagh 60 B2
Inishannon 60 C3
Inishcrone 58 B2
Inveran 60 A2
Irvinestown 59 B4

J

Johnstown 61 B4
Julianstown 59 C5

K

Kanturk 60 B3
Keadew 58 B3
Keady 59 B5
Keel 58 C1
Keenagh 59 C4
Kells
 Antrim 59 B5
 Meath 59 C5
Kenmare 60 C2
Kesh 59 B4
Kilbaha 60 B2
Kilbeggan 61 A4
Kilcock 59 C5
Kilconnell 60 A3
Kilcormac 61 A4
Kilcullen 61 A5
Kilcurry 59 B5
Kildare 61 A5
Kildorrery 60 B3
Kilgarvan 60 C2
Kilkee 60 B2
Kilkeel 59 B5
Kilkelly 58 C3
Kilkenny 61 B4
Kilkieran 60 A2
Kilkinlea 60 B2
Killadysert 60 B2
Killala 58 B2
Killaloe 60 B3
Killarney 60 B2
Killashandra 59 B4
Killashee 59 C4
Killeigh 61 A4
Killenaule 61 B4
Killimor 60 A3
Killinaboy 60 B2

Killinick 61 B5
Killorglin 60 B2
Killucan 59 C4
Killybegs 58 B3
Killyleagh 59 B6
Kilmacrenan 59 A4
Kilmacthomas 61 B4
Kilmaine 58 C2
Kilmallock 60 B3
Kilmeadan 61 B4
Kilmeedy 60 B3
Kilmore Quay 61 B5
Kilnaleck 59 C4
Kilrea 59 B5
Kilrush 60 B2
Kiltoom 58 C3
Kingarrow 58 B3
Kingscourt 59 C5
Kinlough 58 B3
Kinnegad 59 C4
Kinnitty 61 A4
Kinsale 60 C3
Kinvarra 60 A3
Kircubbin 59 B6
Knock 58 C3
Knocktopher 61 B4

L

Laban 60 A3
Lanesborough 59 C4
Laragh 61 A5
Larne 59 B6
Lauragh 60 C2
Laurencetown 60 A3
Leap 60 C2
Leenaun 58 C2
Leighlinbridge 61 B5
Leitrim 58 C3
Letterfrack 58 C2
Letterkenny 59 B4
Lettermacaward 58 B3
Lifford 59 B4
Limavady 59 A5
Limerick 60 B3
Lisbellaw 59 B4
Lisburn 59 B5
Liscannor 60 B2
Lisdoonvarna 60 A2
Lismore 61 B4
Lisnaskea 59 B4
Lissycasey 60 B2
Listowel 60 B3
Littleton 61 B4
Longford 59 C4
Loughbrickland 59 B5
Loughrea 60 A3
Louisburgh 58 C2
Lucan 61 A5
Lurgan 59 B5

M

Macroom 60 C3
Maghera 59 B5
Magherafelt 59 B5
Magilligan 59 A5
Maguiresbridge 59 B4
Malahide 59 C5
Malin 59 A4
Mallaranny 58 C2

Mallow 60 B3
Manorhamilton 58 B3
Markethill 59 B5
Maum 58 C2
Middletown 59 B5
Midleton 60 C3
Milford 59 A4
Millstreet
 Cork 60 B2
 Waterford 61 B4
Milltown
 Galway 58 C3
 Kerry 60 B1
Milltown Malbay . . . 60 B2
Mitchelstown 60 B3
Moate 61 A4
Mohill 59 C4
Monaghan 59 B5
Monasterevin 61 A4
Moneygall 61 B4
Moneymore 59 B5
Mount Bellew 58 C3
Mountbolus 59 B4
Mountmellick 61 A4
Mountrath 61 B4
Moville 59 A4
Moy 59 B5
Moycullen 60 A2
Moylough 58 C3
Muckross 60 B2
Muff 59 A4
Muine Bheag 61 B5
Mullanys Cross 58 B3
Mullinavat 61 B4
Mullingar 59 C4

N

Naas 61 A5
Naul 59 C5
Navan 59 C5
Nenagh 60 B3
Newbliss 59 B4
Newbridge 61 A5
Newcastle 59 B6
Newcastle West 60 B2
Newinn 61 B4
Newmarket 60 B3
Newmarket-on-
 Fergus 60 B3
Newport
 Mayo 58 C2
 Tipperary 60 B3
New Ross 61 B5
Newry 59 B5
Newtownabbey 59 B6
Newtownards 59 B6
Newtownbutler 59 B4
Newtown
 Cunningham 59 B4
Newtownhamilton . . . 59 B5
Newtownmount-
 kennedy 61 A5
Newtown Sands 60 B2
Newtownstewart 59 B4
Ninemilehouse 61 B4

O

Oilgate 61 B5
Oldcastle 59 C4

Omagh 59 B4
Oranmore 60 A3
Oughterard 58 C2

P

Pallas Green 60 B3
Parknasilla 60 C2
Passage East 61 B5
Patrickswell 60 B3
Paulstown 61 B4
Peterswell 60 A3
Pettigo 59 B4
Plumbridge 59 B4
Pomeroy 59 B5
Pontoon 58 C2
Portacloy 58 B2
Portadown 59 B5
Portaferry 59 B6
Portarlington 61 A4
Portavogie 59 B6
Portglenone 59 B5
Portlaoise 61 A4
Portmagne 60 C1
Portroe 60 B3
Portrush 59 A5
Portstewart 59 A5
Portumna 60 A3
Poyntz Pass 59 B5

R

Randalstown 59 B5
Rathangan 61 A5
Rathcoole 61 A5
Rathcormack 60 B3
Rathdrum 61 B5
Rathfriland 59 B5
Rathkeale 60 B3
Rathmelton 59 A4
Rathmolyon 59 C5
Rathmore 60 B2
Rathmullan 59 A4
Rathnew 61 B5
Rathvilly 61 B5
Recess 58 C2
Ringaskiddy 60 C3
Roosky 59 C4
Roscommon 58 C3
Roscrea 61 B4
Rosslare 61 B5
Rosslare Harbour . . . 61 B5
Rosslea 59 B4
Roundwood 61 A5
Rush 59 C5

S

Saintfield 59 B6
Sallins 61 A5
Scarriff 60 B3
Screeb 60 A2
Seskinore 59 B4
Shanagolden 60 B2
Shercock 59 C5
Shillelagh 61 B5
Silvermines 60 B3
Sion Mills 59 B4
Skerries 59 C5
Skibbereen 60 C2

Slane 59 C5
Sligo 58 B3
Sneem 60 C2
Spiddle 60 A2
St. Johnstown 59 B4
Strabane 59 B4
Stradbally 60 B1
Strandhill 58 B3
Strangford 59 B6
Stranorlar 59 B4
Strokestown 58 C3
Swanlinbar 59 B4
Swatragh 59 B5
Swinford 58 C3
Swords 59 C5

T

Tallaght 61 A5
Tallow 60 B3
Tarbert 60 B2
Templederry 60 B3
Templemore 61 B4
Termonfeckin 59 C5
Thomas Street 58 C3
Thomastown 61 B4
Thurles 61 B4
Timoleague 60 C3
Timolin 61 B5
Tipperary 60 B3
Tobermore 59 B5
Toomyvara 60 B3
Toormore 60 C2
Tralee 60 B2
Tramore 61 B4
Trim 59 C5
Tuam 58 C3
Tubbercory 58 B3
Tulla 60 B3
Tullamore 61 A4
Tullow 61 B5
Tulsk 58 C3
Tyrrellspass 61 A4

U

Urlingford 61 B4

V

Virginia 59 C4

W

Warrenpoint 59 B5
Waterford 61 B4
Watergrasshill 60 B3
Waterville 60 C1
Wellingtonbridge . . . 61 B5
Westport 58 C2
Wexford 61 B5
Whitegate 60 C3
Whitehead 59 B6
Wicklow 61 B5

Y

Youghal 61 C4

Index to road maps of Great Britain

How to use the index

Example

Gillingham Dorset **5** A11
- grid square
- page number
- county or unitary authority (only shown for duplicate names)

Abbreviations used in the index

Aberdeen **Aberdeen City**	Flint **Flintshire**	Plym **Plymouth**
Aberds **Aberdeenshire**	Glasgow **City of Glasgow**	Poole **Poole**
Ald **Alderney**	Glos **Gloucestershire**	Powys **Powys**
Anglesey **Isle of Anglesey**	Gtr Man **Greater Manchester**	Ptsmth **Portsmouth**
Angus **Angus**	Guern **Guernsey**	Reading **Reading**
Argyll **Argyll and Bute**	Gwyn **Gwynedd**	Redcar **Redcar and Cleveland**
Bath **Bath and North East Somerset**	Halton **Halton**	Renfs **Renfrewshire**
BCP **Bournemouth, Christchurch**	Hants **Hampshire**	Rhondda **Rhondda Cynon Taff**
and Poole	Hereford **Herefordshire**	Rutland **Rutland**
Bedford **Bedford**	Herts **Hertfordshire**	S Ayrs **South Ayrshire**
Bl Gwent **Blaenau Gwent**	Highld **Highland**	S Glos **South Gloucestershire**
Blackburn **Blackburn with Darwen**	Hrtlpl **Hartlepool**	S Lanark **South Lanarkshire**
Blackpool **Blackpool**	Hull **Hull**	S Yorks **South Yorkshire**
Borders **Scottish Borders**	IoM **Isle of Man**	Scilly **Scilly**
Brack **Bracknell**	IoW **Isle of Wight**	Shetland **Shetland**
Bridgend **Bridgend**	Invclyd **Inverclyde**	Shrops **Shropshire**
Brighton **City of Brighton and Hove**	Jersey **Jersey**	Slough **Slough**
Bristol **City and County of Bristol**	Kent **Kent**	Som **Somerset**
Bucks **Buckinghamshire**	Lancs **Lancashire**	Soton **Southampton**
C Beds **Central Bedfordshire**	Leicester **City of Leicester**	Staffs **Staffordshire**
Caerph **Caerphilly**	Leics **Leicestershire**	Southend **Southend-on-Sea**
Cambs **Cambridgeshire**	Lincs **Lincolnshire**	Stirling **Stirling**
Cardiff **Cardiff**	London **Greater London**	Stockton **Stockton-on-Tees**
Carms **Carmarthenshire**	Luton **Luton**	Stoke **Stoke-on-Trent**
Ceredig **Ceredigion**	M Keynes **Milton Keynes**	Suff **Suffolk**
Ches E **Cheshire East**	M Tydf **Merthyr Tydfil**	Sur **Surrey**
Ches W **Cheshire West and Chester**	Mbro **Middlesbrough**	Swansea **Swansea**
Clack **Clackmannanshire**	Medway **Medway**	Swindon **Swindon**
Conwy **Conwy**	Mers **Merseyside**	T&W **Tyne and Wear**
Corn **Cornwall**	Midloth **Midlothian**	Telford **Telford and Wrekin**
Cumb **Cumbria**	Mon **Monmouthshire**	Thurrock **Thurrock**
Darl **Darlington**	Moray **Moray**	Torbay **Torbay**
Denb **Denbighshire**	N Ayrs **North Ayrshire**	Torf **Torfaen**
Derby **City of Derby**	N Lincs **North Lincolnshire**	V Glam **The Vale of Glamorgan**
Derbys **Derbyshire**	N Lanark **North Lanarkshire**	W Berks **West Berkshire**
Devon **Devon**	N Nhants **North Northamptonshire**	W Dunb **West Dunbartonshire**
Dorset **Dorset**	N Som **North Somerset**	W Isles **Western Isles**
Dumfries **Dumfries and Galloway**	N Yorks **North Yorkshire**	W Loth **West Lothian**
Dundee **Dundee City**	NE Lincs **North East Lincolnshire**	W Mid **West Midlands**
Durham **Durham**	Neath **Neath Port Talbot**	W Nhants **West Northamptonshire**
E Ayrs **East Ayrshire**	Newport **City and County of Newport**	W Sus **West Sussex**
E Dunb **East Dunbartonshire**	Norf **Norfolk**	W Yorks **West Yorkshire**
E Loth **East Lothian**	Northumb **Northumberland**	Warks **Warwickshire**
E Renf **East Renfrewshire**	Nottingham **City of Nottingham**	Warr **Warrington**
E Sus **East Sussex**	Notts **Nottinghamshire**	Wilts **Wiltshire**
E Yorks **East Riding of Yorkshire**	Orkney **Orkney**	Windsor **Windsor and Maidenhead**
Edin **City of Edinburgh**	Oxon **Oxfordshire**	Wokingham **Wokingham**
Essex **Essex**	Pboro **Peterborough**	Worcs **Worcestershire**
Falk **Falkirk**	Pembs **Pembrokeshire**	Wrex **Wrexham**
Fife **Fife**	Perth **Perth and Kinross**	York **City of York**

A

Abbey Town	35 H12
Abbots Bromley	21 D11
Abbotsbury	5 E9
Aberaeron	19 P4
Aberarth	19 P4
Abercarn	7 B11
Aberchirder	50 B5
Abercraf	13 E12
Aberdare	13 F13
Aberdaron	18 H1
Aberdeen	50 G8
Aberdour	40 E4
Aberdulais	13 G11
Aberdyfi	19 L6
Aberfeldy	45 E10
Aberffraw	18 D3
Aberfoyle	44 J7
Abergavenny	14 E1
Abergele	18 C9
Abergwili	12 D8
Abergwyngregyn	18 C6
Abergynolwyn	19 K6
Aberlady	40 E7
Abernethy	40 B4
Aberporth	12 A6
Abersoch	18 H3
Abersychan	7 A11
Abertillery	7 A11
Aberystwyth	19 M5
Abingdon-on-Thames	15 G14
Abington	35 A10
Aboyne	51 H4
Accrington	27 C8
Acha	42 C3
Achanalt	48 B3
Achaphubuil	44 B2
Acharacle	42 B8
Achavanich	53 D13
Achiemore	52 B5
Achiltibuie	52 H2
Achnacroish	42 D10
Achnasheen	48 C2
Achnashellach	46 G10
Achosnich	42 B6
Achriabhach	44 C3
Acklam	33 H9
Acle	24 D8
Acomb	32 J7
Acton Burnell	20 F6
Addingham	32 J2
Adlington	26 D7
Adwick le Street	28 D4
Affric Lodge	48 F2
Ainsdale	26 D4
Aird	43 H9
Aird a Mhulaidh	55 F3
Aird Asaig Tairbeart / Tarbert	55 G3
Airdrie	39 D12
Aird Uig	55 D2
Airor	47 L7
Airth	39 B14
Aisgill	31 E13
Aith	
Orkney	56 D6
Orkney	56 E2
Shetland	57 G4
Akeley	16 B2
Albrighton	21 F9
Alcester	15 A9
Aldborough	32 H6
Aldbourne	15 J11
Aldbrough	29 A11
Aldeburgh	25 K9
Alderbury	8 E6
Alderley Edge	27 H9
Aldermaston	9 A10
Aldershot	9 B13
Aldridge	21 F11
Aldsworth	15 E10
Aldwick	9 H14
Alexandria	39 B8
Alford	
Aberds	50 F4
Lincs	29 G13

Alfreton	28 J3
Alfriston	10 J6
Alkham	11 E13
Allendale Town	36 H7
Allenheads	36 J7
Alloa	39 A13
Allonby	35 J11
Alltforgan	18 H9
Almondsbury	14 H5
Alness	48 B7
Alnmouth	37 B11
Alnwick	37 B10
Alphington	4 E3
Alrewas	21 E12
Alsager	21 A9
Alston	36 J6
Altanduino	53 F10
Altarnun	3 D10
Altass	52 H7
Althorne	17 F14
Althorpe	28 D4
Altnabreac Station	53 D12
Alt na h'Airbhe	52 J3
Altnaharra	52 E7
Alton	
Hants	9 D12
Staffs	21 B11
Altrincham	27 G8
Alva	39 A13
Alvechurch	21 J11
Alveley	21 H8
Alveston	14 H5
Alvie	49 H9
Alwinton	37 C8
Alyth	51 N1
Amble	37 C11
Ambleside	31 D9
Ambrosden	16 D1
Amersham	16 F4
Amesbury	8 C6
Amlwch	18 A4
Ammanford	13 E10
Ampleforth	32 G7
Ampthill	16 B5
Amulree	45 F11
Ancaster	23 A8
Ancroft	41 J12
Ancrum	36 A5
Andover	9 C8
Andoversford	15 E9
Andreas	30 E4
Angle	12 F2
Angmering	10 J1
Annan	35 G12
Annbank	34 A5
Annfield Plain	37 H10
Anstey	22 E4
Anstruther	41 C8
An t-Ob / Leverburgh	55 J2
Appleby-in-Westmorland	31 B12
Applecross	46 G7
Appledore	
Devon	6 J3
Kent	11 G10
Arboath	51 N5
Archiestown	49 D13
Ardarroch	46 G8
Ardbeg	43 P6
Ardcharnich	52 K3
Ardchyle	44 G7
Ardentinny	38 B6
Ardersier	49 C8
Ardessie	52 K2
Ardgay	52 J7
Ardhasig	55 G3
Ardingly	10 G4
Ardlamont Ho.	38 D4
Ardleigh	25 N5
Ardley	15 D14
Ardlui	44 H5
Ardlussa	43 K8
Ardnave	43 L4
Ardrishaig	38 B3
Ardrossan	38 F7
Ardtalla	43 N6
Ardtalnaig	45 F9
Ardtoe	42 A8

Ardvasar	47 L6
Ardwell	
Dumfries	34 J2
Moray	50 E2
Arileod	42 C3
Arinagour	42 C4
Arisaig	47 N6
Armadale	
Highland	47 L6
W Loth	40 G2
Armathwaite	36 J4
Armitage	21 E11
Armthorpe	28 D5
Arncliffe	32 G1
Arncott	16 D1
Arnisdale	47 K8
Arnold	22 A4
Arreton	9 J10
Arrochar	44 J5
Arundel	10 J1
Ascot	16 J4
Asfordby	22 C6
Ash	
Kent	11 D13
Sur	9 C13
Ashbourne	21 B12
Ashburton	4 G1
Ashbury	15 H11
Ashby de-la-Zouch	22 D2
Ashchurch	15 C8
Ashford	
Derbys	27 J12
Kent	11 E11
Ashingdon	17 F13
Ashington	37 E11
Ashley	21 C8
Ashton	26 J5
Ashton-in-Makerfield	26 F6
Ashton Keynes	15 G9
Ashton under Hill	15 C9
Ashton under Lyne	27 F10
Ashurst	9 G8
Ashwater	3 B11
Ashwell	16 B7
Ashwick	8 C1
Askam-in-Furness	31 G8
Askern	28 C4
Askrigg	32 E1
Aspatria	35 J12
Astwood Bank	21 K11
Atherstone	22 F2
Atherton	26 E7
Attleborough	24 F5
Atworth	8 A3
Auchduart	52 H2
Auchenblae	51 J6
Auchencairn	35 H8
Auchengray	40 H3
Auchertool	40 D5
Auchinleck	34 A6
Auchronie	51 J3
Auchterarder	45 H11
Auchterderran	40 D5
Auchtermuchty	40 B5
Auchtertyre	47 J8
Audlem	20 B7
Audley	21 A8
Auldearn	49 C10
Aultbea	46 C8
Austwick	31 H13
Avebury	15 K10
Avening	14 G7
Aveton Gifford	3 G14
Aviemore	49 G9
Avoch	48 C8
Avonmouth	14 J4
Axbridge	7 F13
Axminster	4 D6
Axmouth	4 E6
Aylesbury	16 D3
Aylesford	11 D8
Aylesham	11 D13
Aylsham	24 C6
Ayr	34 A4
Aysgarth	32 F1
Ayton	
Borders	41 G12

Ayton continued	
N Yorks	33 F11

B

Bac	55 C6
Backwell	7 E13
Bacton	24 B8
Bacup	27 C9
Badenscoth	50 D6
Badenyon	50 F2
Badminton	14 H7
Badrallach	52 J2
Bagh a Chaisteil / Castlebay	54 K3
Bagillt	26 H3
Bagshot	16 J4
Baildon	27 B12
Baile	54 A6
Baile Ailein	55 E5
Baile Mhartainn	54 B4
Bainbridge	32 E1
Bainton	33 J11
Bakewell	27 J13
Bala	18 G9
Balbeggie	45 F13
Balblair	49 B8
Balcombe	10 G4
Balderton	28 J7
Baldock	16 B7
Balephuil	42 D1
Balfour	56 E4
Balfron	39 B10
Balintore	49 A9
Ballachulish	44 D2
Ballantrae	34 E2
Ballasalla	30 H2
Ballater	51 H2
Ballaugh	30 F3
Ballinaby	43 M4
Ballinluig	45 D11
Balloch	
Highland	49 D8
W Dunb	39 B8
Ballochan	51 H4
Ballygrant	43 M5
Ballyhaugh	42 C3
Balmacellan	34 F7
Balmedie	50 F8
Balnacoil	53 H10
Balnapaling	49 B8
Balquhidder	44 G7
Balsall	21 J13
Balsham	23 K14
Baltasound	57 A7
Balvicar	42 G9
Bamber Bridge	26 C6
Bamburgh	41 K14
Bamford	27 G13
Bampton	
Devon	4 A3
Oxon	15 F12
Banbury	15 C13
Banchory	51 H5
Banff	50 A5
Bangor	18 C5
Bangor-is-y-coed	20 B5
Banham	24 G5
Bankend	35 G11
Bankfoot	45 F12
Bankhead	50 F7
Banks	26 C4
Bannockburn	39 A13
Banstead	10 D3
Banwell	7 F12
Barabhas	55 B5
Barassie	39 E5
Barbon	31 F12
Bardney	29 H10
Barford	22 J1
Bargoed	7 B10
Bargrennan	34 F4
Barham	11 D13
Bar Hill	23 J12
Barkway	17 B8
Barlborough	28 G3
Barlby	28 A5
Barley	17 B9

Barmby Moor	33 K9
Barmoor Castle	41 J12
Barmouth	19 J6
Barnard Castle	32 C2
Barnet	16 F7
Barnetby le Wold	29 D9
Barnham	24 H3
Barnhill	49 C12
Barnoldswick	27 A9
Barnsley	28 D2
Barnstaple	6 H4
Barnt Green	21 J11
Barr	34 D3
Barrhead	39 E9
Barrhill	34 E3
Barrowford	27 B9
Barrow-in-Furness	30 G7
Barrow upon Humber	29 B9
Barry	
Angus	51 P4
V Glam	7 E10
Barton	32 D4
Barton-le-Clay	16 C5
Barton upon Humber	29 B9
Barwell	22 F3
Baschurch	20 D5
Basildon	17 G12
Basingstoke	9 B11
Baslow	27 H13
Baston	23 D10
Bath	8 A2
Bathford	8 A2
Bathgate	40 G2
Batley	27 C13
Battle	11 H8
Bawdeswell	24 C5
Bawdsey	25 L8
Bawtry	28 E5
Bayston Hill	20 F5
Beachley	14 G4
Beaconsfield	16 G4
Beadnell	37 A11
Beaminster	5 D8
Bearsden	39 C10
Bearsted	11 D8
Beattock	35 C11
Beaufort	13 E15
Beaulieu	9 G8
Beauly	48 D6
Beaumaris	18 C5
Bebington	26 G4
Beccles	24 F9
Beckermet	30 D6
Beckfoot	35 J11
Beckhampton	15 K10
Beckingham	28 E6
Beckington	8 B3
Beck Row	24 H1
Bedale	32 F4
Beddgelert	18 F5
Bedford	16 A5
Bedlington	37 E11
Bedwas	7 C10
Bedworth	22 G2
Beeford	33 J13
Beer	4 E6
Beeston	22 B4
Beeswing	35 G9
Begelly	12 F5
Beguildy	20 J3
Beighton	28 F3
Beith	39 E8
Belbroughton	21 J10
Belchford	29 G11
Belford	41 K14
Bellingham	36 E7
Bellsbank	34 C5
Bellshill	39 D12
Belmont	
Blackburn	26 D7
Shetland	57 B6
Belper	28 K2
Belsay	37 F9
Beltinge	11 C12

Belton
N Lincs 28 D6
Norf 24 E9
Bembridge 9 J11
Benington 23 A12
Benllech 18 B5
Benson 16 F1
Bentley
Hants 9 C12
S Yorks 28 D4
Benwick 23 F12
Bere Alston 3 E12
Bere Regis 8 H3
Berkeley 14 G5
Berkhamsted 16 E4
Berriedale 53 F13
Berriew 20 F2
Berrow 7 F11
Berwick 10 J6
Berwick-upon-Tweed 41 H12
Bethersden 11 F10
Bethesda 18 D6
Bettws Bledrws 19 Q6
Bettyhill 53 B9
Betws 13 H13
Betws-y-Coed 18 E7
Beulah 13 A13
Beverley 29 A9
Bewcastle 36 F4
Bewdley 21 J8
Bexhill 11 J8
Bexley 10 B5
Bibury 15 F10
Bicester 15 D14
Bickington 4 F1
Bicton 20 E5
Biddenden 11 F9
Biddulph 27 K9
Bideford 6 J3
Bidford-on-Avon 15 A10
Bigbury on Sea 3 G14
Biggar 40 K3
Biggin Hill 10 D5
Biggleswade 16 A7
Bildeston 25 L4
Billericay 17 F11
Billesdon 22 E6
Billingborough 23 B10
Billingham 32 B6
Billinghay 29 J10
Billingshurst 10 G1
Bilston 21 G10
Binbrook 29 E11
Bingham 22 B5
Bingley 27 B12
Birchgrove 13 G10
Birchington 11 C14
Birdlip 15 E8
Birkdale 26 D4
Birkenhead 26 G4
Birmingham 21 H11
Birtley
Northumb 36 F7
T&W 37 H11
Bishop Auckland 32 B4
Bishopbriggs 39 C11
Bishop Monkton 32 H5
Bishop's Castle 20 H4
Bishop's Cleeve 15 D8
Bishop's Frome 14 B5
Bishops Lydeard 7 J10
Bishop's Nympton 6 J6
Bishop's Stortford 17 C9
Bishop's Tawton 6 J4
Bishopsteignton 4 F3
Bishopstoke 9 F9
Bishopston 13 H9
Bishop's Waltham 9 F10
Bitton 14 K5
Blaby 22 F4
Blackburn 26 C7
Blackfield 9 G9
Blackford
Cumb 36 G2
Perth 45 J11
Blackpool 26 B4
Blackridge 39 D13
Blackwall Tunnel 10 B4
Blackwaterfoot 38 H4
Blackwood
Caerph 7 B10
S Lanark 39 F12
Blaenau Ffestiniog 18 F7
Blaenavon 14 F1
Blaengraw 13 G13
Blagdon 7 F14
Blaina 7 A11
Blair Atholl 45 C10
Blairgowrie 45 E13
Blakeney
Glos 14 F5
Norf 24 A5
Blanchand 37 H8
Blandford Forum 8 G3
Blaydon 37 G10
Bleadon 7 F12
Blean 11 D12
Bletchingdon 15 E14
Bletchley 16 B3
Blewbury 15 H14
Blidworth 28 J5
Blindburn 36 B7
Blisworth 22 K6
Blockley 15 C10
Blofield 24 D8
Bloxham 15 C13
Blubberhouses 32 J3
Blundeston 24 F10
Blyth
Northumb 37 E12
Notts 28 F5
Blyth Bridge 40 J4
Blythburgh 25 H9
Blythe Bridge 21 B10
Blyton 28 E7
Boath 48 A6
Boat of Garten 49 G10
Boddam
Aberds 50 C10
Shetland 57 L5
Bodedern 18 C3
Bodenham 14 A4
Bodiam 11 G8
Bodinnick 3 F9
Bodmin 3 E8
Bognor Regis 9 H14
Boldon 37 G12
Bollington 27 H10
Bolney 10 G3
Bolsover 28 G3
Bolton 27 E8
Bolton Abbey 32 J2
Bolton Bridge 32 J2
Bolton by Bowland 31 K13
Bolton le Sands 31 H10
Bonarbridge 52 J8
Bonawe 44 F2
Bonby 29 C8
Bonchester Bridge 36 B4
Bonchurch 9 K10
Bo'ness 40 E2
Bonhill 39 B9
Bonnybridge 39 B13
Bonnyrigg 40 G6
Bonvilston 7 D9
Boot 30 D7
Bootle
Cumb 30 F7
Mers 26 F4
Bordon 9 D13
Borehamwood 16 F6
Boreland 35 D12
Borgh 55 B6
Borgue 34 J7
Boroughbridge 32 H5
Borough Green 10 D7
Borrowdale 31 C8
Borth 19 M6
Bosbury 14 B6
Boscastle 3 C8
Bosham 9 G13
Boston 23 A12
Boston Spa 32 K6
Botesdale 24 H5
Bothel 35 J12
Bothenhampton 5 E8
Botley 15 F13
Bottesford 22 B7
Bottisham 23 J14
Botwnnog 18 G2
Boughton 28 H5
Bourne 23 C9
Bourne End 16 G4
Bournemouth 8 H5
Bourton-on-the-Water 15 D10
Bovey Tracey 4 F2
Bow 4 D1
Bowes 32 C2
Bowmore 43 N5
Bowness-on-Solway 35 G13
Bowness-on-Windermere 31 E10
Box 14 K7
Bozeat 23 K8
Brabourne 11 E11
Brabourne Lees 11 F11
Bracadale 47 H3
Bracebridge Heath 29 H8
Bracklesham 9 H13
Brackley
W Nhants 15 C15
W Nhants 16 B1
Bracknell 16 J3
Braco 45 J10
Bradford 27 B12
Bradford-on-Avon 8 A3
Brading 9 J11
Bradpole 5 D8
Bradwell Waterside 25 Q5
Bradworthy 6 K2
Brae 57 F4
Braeantra 48 A6
Braemar 49 J12
Braemore
Highland 48 A3
Highland 53 F12
Brae Roy Lodge 48 J4
Brailsford 21 B13
Braintree 17 C12
Bramford 25 L6
Bramhall 27 G9
Bramhope 27 A13
Brampton
Cambs 23 H11
Cumb 36 G4
Brancaster 24 A2
Branderburgh 49 A13
Brandon
Durham 37 J11
Suff 24 G2
Branston 29 H9
Brantham 25 M6
Bratton Fleming 6 H5
Braunston 22 J4
Braunton 6 H3
Bray 16 H4
Breage 2 J4
Breakish 47 J6
Bream 14 F5
Breanais 55 E2
Brechfa 13 C9
Brechin 51 L5
Breck of Cruan 56 E3
Brecon 13 D14
Brede 11 H9
Bredenbury 14 A5
Bremirehoull 57 K5
Brent 10 A3
Brentwood 17 F11
Bretforton 15 B9
Brewood 21 F9
Bride 30 E4
Bridestowe 3 C13
Bridge 11 D12
Bridgend
Argyll 43 M5
Bridgend 13 J13
Bridge of Allan 39 A12
Bridge of Balgie 44 E7
Bridge of Cally 45 D13
Bridge of Don 50 F8
Bridge of Earn 45 H13
Bridge of Orchy 44 E5
Bridge of Weir 39 D8
Bridgnorth 21 G8
Bridgwater 7 H12
Bridlington 33 H13
Bridport 5 D8
Brierfield 27 B9
Brierley Hill 21 H10
Brigg 29 D9
Brighouse 27 C12
Brighstone 9 J9
Brightlingsea 25 P5
Brighton 10 J4
Brigstock 23 G8
Brill 16 D1
Brimfield 20 K6
Brinian 56 D4
Brinklow 22 H3
Brinkworth 15 H9
Bristol 14 J4
Briston 24 B5
Briton Ferry 13 G11
Brixham 4 H3
Brixton 3 F13
Brixworth 22 H6
Brize Norton 15 F11
Broad Chalke 8 E5
Broadclyst 4 D3
Broadford 47 J6
Broad Haven 12 E2
Broadhembury 4 C4
Broad Hinton 15 J10
Broadmayne 5 E11
Broadstairs 11 C15
Broadstone 8 H4
Broadwas 14 A6
Broadway 15 C10
Broadwey 5 E10
Broadwindsor 5 C8
Brochel 46 G5
Brockenhurst 9 G8
Brockworth 15 E8
Brocton 21 E10
Brodick 38 G5
Bromfield 20 J5
Bromham
Bedford 23 K8
Wilts 8 A4
Bromley 10 C5
Bromley Green 11 F10
Brompton 32 E5
Brompton Regis 4 A3
Bromsgrove 21 J10
Bromyard 14 A5
Brooke 24 F7
Broomfield 17 D12
Broomhaugh 37 G9
Broomhill 37 C11
Brora 53 H10
Broseley 20 F7
Brothertoft 29 K11
Brotton 33 B8
Brough
Cumb 31 C14
E Yorks 29 B8
Highland 53 A14
Shetland 57 E5
Broughton
Borders 40 K4
Hants 9 D8
Lancs 26 B6
N Lincs 29 D8
N Nhants 22 H7
Broughton Astley 22 F4
Broughton-in-Furness 31 F8
Broughty Ferry 51 P3
Brownhills 21 F11
Broxburn 40 F3
Broxton 20 A5
Bruichladdich 43 M4
Brundall 24 E8
Brunton
Northumb 37 A11
Northumb 37 F8
Bruton 8 D1
Brymbo 20 A3
Brynamman 13 E11
Bryncrug 19 K6
Brynmawr 13 E15
Brynsiencyn 18 D4
Bubwith 28 A6
Buchlyvie 39 A10
Buckden
Cambs 23 J10
N Yorks 32 G1
Buckfast 4 G1
Buckfastleigh 4 G1
Buckhaven 40 D6
Buckie 50 A3
Buckingham 16 B2
Buckland 15 G12
Buckland Brewer 6 K3
Buckland Newton 5 C10
Buckley 26 J3
Bucksburn 50 F8
Buck's Cross 6 J2
Bude 3 A10
Budleigh Salterton 4 F4
Bugbrooke 22 K5
Bugle 3 F8
Builth Wells 13 A14
Bulford 8 C6
Bulkington 22 G2
Bulwell 22 A4
Bunbury 26 K6
Bunessan 42 F5
Bungay 24 G8
Bunnahabhain 43 L6
Buntingford 17 C8
Bunwell 24 F6
Burbage
Derbys 27 H11
Leics 22 F3
Wilts 8 B7
Bures 25 M4
Burford 15 E11
Burgess Hill 10 H4
Burgh-by-Sands 36 H2
Burghclere 9 A9
Burghead 49 B12
Burghfield Common 16 J1
Burgh le Marsh 29 H14
Burley
Hants 8 G7
W Yorks 32 K3
Burlton 20 D5
Burneside 31 E11
Burness 56 B6
Burnham 16 G4
Burnham Market 24 A3
Burnham-on-Crouch 17 F14
Burnham-on-Sea 7 G12
Burniston 33 E12
Burnley 27 B9
Burnmouth 41 G12
Burntisland 40 E5
Burntwood 21 F11
Burrafirth 57 A7
Burravoe 57 D6
Burrelton 45 F14
Burry Port
Carms 12 G8
Carms 13 G8
Burscough Bridge 26 D5
Burstwick 29 B11
Burton 31 G11
Burton Agnes 33 H13
Burton Bradstock 5 E8
Burton Fleming 33 G12
Burton in Lonsdale 31 G12
Burton Latimer 22 H7
Burton upon Stather 28 C7
Burton upon Trent 21 D13
Burwash 10 G7
Burwell 23 J14
Burwick 56 H4
Bury 27 E9
Bury St Edmunds 25 J3
Bushey 16 F6
Buttermere 30 C7
Buxted 10 G6
Buxton 27 H11
Byfield 15 A14
Byfleet 16 J5
Bylchau 18 D9

Cabrach . . . 50 E2
Caenby Corner . . . 29 F8
Caergwrle . . . 20 A4
Caerleon . . . 7 C12
Caernarfon . . . 18 D4
Caerphilly . . . 7 C10
Caersws . . . 19 L10
Caerwent . . . 14 G3
Cairinis . . . 54 C5
Cairndow . . . 44 H3
Cairngaan . . . 34 K2
Cairnryan . . . 34 G1
Caister-on-Sea . . . 24 D10
Caistor . . . 29 D10
Calanais . . . 55 D4
Caldbeck . . . 36 J2
Calder Bridge . . . 30 D6
Caldercruix . . . 39 D13
Caldicot . . . 14 H3
Calfsound . . . 56 C5
Calgary . . . 42 C5
Callander . . . 45 J8
Callington . . . 3 E11
Calne . . . 15 J9
Calshot . . . 9 H9
Calstock . . . 3 E12
Calverton . . . 28 K5
Cam . . . 14 G6
Camber . . . 11 H10
Camberley . . . 16 K3
Cambo . . . 37 E9
Camborne . . . 2 H4
Cambourne . . . 23 K12
Cambridge . . . 23 K13
Camden . . . 10 A3
Camelford . . . 3 C9
Cammachmore . . . 51 H8
Campbeltown . . . 38 H2
Camrose . . . 12 E3
Canisbay . . . 53 A15
Cannich . . . 48 E4
Cannington . . . 7 H11
Cannock . . . 21 F10
Canonbie . . . 36 F2
Canterbury . . . 11 D12
Cantley . . . 24 E8
Canvey Island . . . 17 G13
Caol . . . 44 B3
Caolas Stocinis . . . 55 H3
Caoles . . . 42 D2
Capel . . . 10 F2
Capel Curig . . . 18 E7
Capel St Mary . . . 25 M6
Carbis Bay . . . 2 H3
Carbost
  Highland . . . 46 G4
  Highland . . . 47 H3
Cardiff . . . 7 D10
Cardigan . . . 12 B5
Cardington . . . 16 A5
Cardross . . . 39 C8
Cargill . . . 45 F13
Carhampton . . . 7 G9
Carisbrooke . . . 9 J9
Cark . . . 31 G9
Carlabhagh . . . 55 C4
Carleton Rode . . . 24 F6
Carlisle . . . 36 H3
Carlops . . . 40 H4
Carlton
  Notts . . . 22 A5
  N Yorks . . . 28 B5
Carlton Colville . . . 24 G10
Carlton-in-Lindrick . 28 F4
Carlton Miniott . . . 32 F6
Carluke . . . 39 E13
Carmarthen . . . 12 E8
Carmyllie . . . 51 N4
Carnachuin . . . 49 J9
Carnforth . . . 31 G11
Carno . . . 19 L9
Carnoustie . . . 51 P4
Carnwath . . . 40 J2
Carradale . . . 38 G3
Carrbridge . . . 49 F10
Carrick . . . 38 A7

Carronbridge . . . 35 D9
Carsaig . . . 42 F7
Carskiey . . . 38 K1
Carsphairn . . . 34 D6
Carstairs . . . 40 J3
Carterton . . . 15 F11
Cartmel . . . 31 G9
Castle Acre . . . 24 D3
Castlebay / Bagh a
  Chaisteil . . . 54 K3
Castle Cary . . . 8 D1
Castle Donington . . 22 C3
Castle Douglas . . . 35 G8
Castleford . . . 28 B3
Castlemartin . . . 12 G3
Castleside . . . 37 J9
Castleton
  Derbys . . . 27 G12
  N Yorks . . . 33 D10
Castletown
  Highland . . . 53 B14
  IoM . . . 30 J2
Caston . . . 24 F4
Castor . . . 23 F10
Catcleugh . . . 36 C6
Caterham . . . 10 D4
Caton . . . 31 H11
Catrine . . . 39 H10
Catsfield . . . 11 H8
Catterall . . . 26 A6
Catterick . . . 32 E4
Catterick Camp . . . 32 E3
Catton . . . 36 H7
Caulkerbush . . . 35 H10
Cawdor . . . 49 C9
Cawood . . . 28 A4
Cawston . . . 24 C6
Caythorpe . . . 29 K8
Ceann Tarabhaigh . . 55 F4
Cefn-mawr . . . 20 B3
Cemaes . . . 18 A3
Cemaes Road . . . 19 K8
Cenarth . . . 12 B6
Ceres . . . 40 B7
Cerne Abbas . . . 5 C10
Cerrigydrudion . . . 18 F9
Chacewater . . . 2 G5
Chaddesley Corbet . 21 J9
Chadwell St Mary . . 17 H11
Chagford . . . 3 C14
Chalfont St Giles . . 16 F4
Chalford . . . 15 F8
Chalgrove . . . 16 F1
Challacombe . . . 6 H5
Challock . . . 11 E11
Chandler's Ford . . . 9 F12
Channel Tunnel . . . 11 F12
Chapel en le Frith . . 27 G11
Chapel St Leonards 29 G14
Chapeltown
  S Lanark . . . 39 F11
  S Yorks . . . 28 E2
Chard . . . 4 C7
Charing . . . 11 E10
Charlbury . . . 15 E12
Charlestown of
  Aberlour . . . 49 D13
Charlton . . . 15 H8
Charlton Horethorne 5 A10
Charlton Kings . . . 15 E8
Charlwood . . . 10 E3
Charminster . . . 5 D10
Charmouth . . . 4 D7
Chartham . . . 11 D12
Chatham . . . 17 J12
Chathill . . . 37 A10
Chatteris . . . 23 G12
Chatton . . . 37 A9
Chawleigh . . . 4 C1
Cheadle
  Grt Manchester . . 27 G9
  Staffs . . . 21 B11
Chedburgh . . . 25 K2
Cheddar . . . 7 F13
Cheddleton . . . 21 A10
Chellaston . . . 22 B2
Chelmarsh . . . 21 H8
Chelmsford . . . 17 E12
Cheltenham . . . 15 D8

Chepstow . . . 14 G4
Cherhill . . . 15 K9
Cheriton . . . 9 E11
Cheriton Fitzpaine . . 4 C2
Chertsey . . . 16 J5
Chesham . . . 16 E4
Cheshunt . . . 17 E8
Chester . . . 26 J5
Chesterfield . . . 28 G2
Chester-le-Street . . 37 H11
Chew Magna . . . 7 E14
Chewton Mendip . . 7 F14
Chichester . . . 9 G13
Chiddingfold . . . 9 D14
Chideock . . . 5 D8
Chigwell . . . 17 F9
Chilcompton . . . 8 B1
Chilham . . . 11 D11
Chillington . . . 4 J1
Chilton . . . 32 A4
Chingford . . . 17 F8
Chinnor . . . 16 E2
Chippenham . . . 15 J8
Chipping Campden .15 C10
Chipping Norton . . 15 D12
Chipping Ongar . . . 17 E10
Chipping Sodbury . . 14 H6
Chirbury . . . 20 G3
Chirk . . . 20 C3
Chirnside . . . 41 H11
Chiseldon . . . 15 J10
Chitterne . . . 8 C4
Chobham . . . 16 J4
Chollerton . . . 37 F8
Cholsey . . . 15 H14
Chorley . . . 26 D6
Chorleywood . . . 16 F5
Christchurch
  BCP . . . 8 H6
  Cambs . . . 23 F13
Christow . . . 4 E2
Chudleigh . . . 4 F2
Chulmleigh . . . 6 K5
Churchdown . . . 14 E7
Churchill . . . 15 D11
Churchstow . . . 4 J1
Church Stretton . . 20 G5
Church Village . . . 7 C9
Chwilog . . . 18 G4
Cilgerran . . . 12 B5
Cille Bhrighde . . . 54 H4
Cilycwm . . . 13 C11
Cinderford . . . 14 E5
Cirencester . . . 15 F9
City of London . . . 10 A4
Clachan
  Argyll . . . 38 E3
  Highland . . . 47 H5
Clachan na Luib . . 54 C5
Clackmannan . . . 40 D2
Clacton-on-Sea . . 25 P6
Cladich . . . 44 G2
Claggan . . . 42 D9
Claigan . . . 46 F2
Clanfield . . . 9 F12
Claonaig . . . 38 E3
Clapham
  Bedford . . . 23 K9
  N Yorks . . . 31 H13
Clare . . . 25 L2
Clashmore . . . 53 K9
Clavering . . . 17 C9
Claverley . . . 21 G8
Clawton . . . 3 B11
Clay Cross . . . 28 H2
Claydon . . . 25 K6
Claypole . . . 28 K7
Cleadale . . . 47 N4
Cleat . . . 56 H4
Cleator Moor . . . 30 C6
Cleethorpes . . . 29 D11
Cleeve Prior . . . 15 A10
Clehonger . . . 14 C3
Cleobury Mortimer . 20 J3
Clevedon . . . 7 D13
Cleveleys . . . 26 A4
Cley . . . 24 A5
Cliffe . . . 17 H12
Clifford . . . 14 B1

Clipston . . . 22 G6
Clipstone . . . 28 H4
Clitheroe . . . 27 A8
Clive . . . 20 D6
Clophill . . . 16 B5
Closeburn . . . 35 D9
Cloughton . . . 33 E12
Clova . . . 51 K2
Clovelly . . . 6 J2
Clovenfords . . . 40 K7
Clowne . . . 28 G3
Clun . . . 20 H4
Clunbury . . . 20 H4
Clunes . . . 48 K3
Clungunford . . . 20 J4
Clutton . . . 8 B1
Clydach . . . 13 F10
Clydebank . . . 39 D10
Clynnog-fawr . . . 18 F4
Clyro . . . 14 B1
Coalbrookdale . . . 20 F7
Coalburn . . . 39 G13
Coalville . . . 22 D3
Coatbridge . . . 39 D12
Cobham
  Kent . . . 17 J11
  Sur . . . 10 D2
Cock Bridge . . . 49 G13
Cockburnspath . . . 41 F10
Cockenzie . . . 40 F7
Cockerham . . . 31 J10
Cockermouth . . . 30 A7
Cockfield
  Durham . . . 32 B3
  Suff . . . 25 K4
Cockshutt . . . 20 D5
Coddenham . . . 25 K6
Codford St Mary . . 8 D4
Coggeshall . . . 25 N3
Coignafearn Lodge . 48 G7
Coille Mhorgil . . . 48 H1
Coillore . . . 47 H3
Colby . . . 30 J2
Colchester . . . 25 N5
Cold Ashton . . . 14 J6
Coldingham . . . 41 E10
Coldstream . . . 41 J11
Coleford
  Devon . . . 4 D1
  Glos . . . 14 F4
Coleshill . . . 21 H13
Colinton . . . 40 G5
Colintraive . . . 38 C5
Collieston . . . 50 E9
Collin . . . 35 F11
Collingbourne
  Kingston . . . 8 B7
Collingham
  Notts . . . 28 H7
  W Yorks . . . 32 K5
Colmonel . . . 34 E2
Colne . . . 27 B10
Colpy . . . 50 D5
Colsterworth . . . 23 C8
Coltishall . . . 24 C7
Colwell . . . 37 F8
Colwich . . . 21 D11
Colwyn Bay . . . 18 C8
Colyton . . . 4 D6
Combe Martin . . . 6 G4
Comberton . . . 23 K12
Combwich . . . 7 G11
Compton
  W Berks . . . 15 J14
  W Sus . . . 9 F12
Compton Martin . . 7 F14
Comrie . . . 45 G9
Condover . . . 20 F5
Congresbury . . . 7 E13
Coningsby . . . 29 J11
Conisbrough . . . 28 E4
Coniston . . . 31 E8
Connah's Quay . . . 26 J3
Connel . . . 44 F1
Connel Park . . . 34 B7
Cononbridge . . . 48 C6
Consett . . . 37 H10
Contin . . . 48 C5

Conwy . . . 18 C7
Cookham . . . 16 G4
Coolham . . . 10 G2
Coombe Bissett . . 8 E6
Copplestone . . . 4 C1
Coppull . . . 26 D6
Copthorne . . . 10 F4
Corbridge . . . 37 G8
Corby . . . 22 G7
Corby Glen . . . 23 C9
Corfe Castle . . . 8 J4
Corfe Mullen . . . 8 H4
Cornhill on Tweed . . 41 K11
Corpach . . . 44 B2
Corran . . . 44 C2
Corrie . . . 38 F5
Corringham
  Lincs . . . 28 E7
  Thurrock . . . 17 G12
Corris . . . 19 K7
Corsham . . . 14 J7
Corsley . . . 8 C3
Corsock . . . 35 F8
Corton . . . 24 F10
Corwen . . . 18 F10
Coryton . . . 17 G12
Coseley . . . 21 G10
Cosham . . . 9 G11
Costessey . . . 24 D6
Cotgrave . . . 22 B5
Cotherstone . . . 32 B2
Cottenham . . . 23 J13
Cottered . . . 17 C8
Cottesmore . . . 23 D8
Cottingham . . . 29 A9
Coulags . . . 46 G9
Coulport . . . 38 B7
Countesthorpe . . . 22 F4
Coupar Angus . . . 45 E14
Cove
  Argyll . . . 38 B7
  Highland . . . 46 B8
Cove Bay . . . 50 G8
Coventry . . . 22 H2
Coverack . . . 2 K5
Cowbit . . . 23 D11
Cowbridge . . . 13 J13
Cowdenbeath . . . 40 D4
Cowes . . . 9 H9
Cowfold . . . 10 G3
Cowpen . . . 37 E11
Cowplain . . . 9 F11
Coxheath . . . 11 D8
Coylton . . . 34 A5
Craggie . . . 49 E8
Crai . . . 13 D12
Craibstone . . . 50 B3
Craigellachie . . . 49 D13
Craighouse . . . 43 M7
Craigmore . . . 38 D6
Craignure . . . 42 E9
Craigtown . . . 53 C11
Crail . . . 41 C9
Cramlington . . . 37 F11
Cranborne . . . 8 F5
Cranbrook
  Devon . . . 4 D4
  Kent . . . 11 F8
Cranleigh . . . 10 F1
Cranmore . . . 8 C1
Cranstal . . . 30 E4
Cranwell . . . 29 K9
Crathie . . . 49 J13
Craven Arms . . . 20 H5
Crawford . . . 35 A10
Crawfordjohn . . . 39 H13
Crawley . . . 10 F3
Creag Ghoraidh . . 54 E5
Creake . . . 24 B3
Credenhill . . . 14 B3
Crediton . . . 4 D2
Creetown . . . 34 H5
Cressage . . . 20 F7
Cresselly . . . 12 F4
Crewe . . . 21 A8
Crewkerne . . . 5 C8

Crianlarich 44 G5
Criccieth 18 G5
Crick 22 H4
Crickhowell 14 E1
Cricklade 15 G10
Crieff 45 G10
Crimond 50 B9
Crinan 38 A2
Crocketford 35 F9
Croggan 42 F9
Croglin 36 J4
Croick 52 J6
Cromarty 49 B8
Cromer 24 A7
Cromor 55 E6
Crondall 9 C12
Crook 37 K10
Crookham 41 K12
Crooklands 31 F11
Crosbost 55 E6
Crosby 35 J11
Crosby Ravensworth 31 C12
Cross-Hands 13 E9
Crosshill 34 C4
Crossmichael 35 G8
Croston 26 D5
Crowborough 10 F6
Crowland 23 D11
Crowle 28 C6
Crowthorne 16 J3
Croxton Kerrial 22 C7
Croyde 6 H3
Croydon 10 C4
Cruden Bay 50 D9
Crudgington 20 E7
Crulabhig 55 D3
Crymych 12 C5
Cuaig 46 F7
Cuan 42 G9
Cuckfield 10 G4
Cuddington
- Bucks 16 D2
- Ches W 26 H6
Cudworth 28 C2
Cuffley 17 E8
Culgaith 31 A12
Culkein 52 E2
Cullen 50 A4
Cullicudden 48 B7
Cullivoe 57 B6
Culloden 49 D8
Cullompton 4 C4
Culmazie 34 H4
Culmington 20 H5
Culmstock 4 B5
Culrain 52 J7
Cults 50 G7
Cumbernauld 39 C12
Cuminestown 50 B7
Cummertrees 35 G12
Cumnock 34 A6
Cumnor 15 F13
Cumwhinton 36 H3
Cupar 40 B6
Currie 40 G4
Curry Rivel 7 J12
Cwmafan 13 G11
Cwmann 13 B9
Cwmbran 7 B11
Cwrt 19 K7
Cymmer 13 G12
Cynwyl Elfed 12 D7

D

Dagenham 17 G10
Dail bho Dheas 55 A6
Dailly 34 C3
Dalabrog 54 G4
Dalbeattie 35 G9
Dale 12 F2
Dale of Walls 57 G2
Dalguise 45 E11
Dalhalvaig 53 C11
Dalkeith 40 G6
Dallas 49 C12
Dalleagles 34 B6
Dalmally 44 G3
Dalmellington 34 C5
Dalnaspidal 45 B8
Dalnessie 52 G8
Dalry 38 F7
Dalrymple 34 B4
Dalston 36 H2
Dalton
- Dumfries 35 F12
- Northumb 37 H8
- N Yorks 32 D5
Dalton-in-Furness 31 G8
Dalwhinnie 45 A8
Damerham 8 F6
Danbury 17 E13
Darlington 32 C4
Dartford 17 H10
Dartford Crossing 17 H10
Dartington 4 G1
Dartmouth 4 H2
Darton 28 C2
Darvel 39 G10
Darwen 26 C7
Daventry 22 J4
Davington 35 C13
Dawlish 4 F3
Deal 11 D14
Dearham 35 K11
Dearne 28 D3
Debenham 25 J6
Deddington 15 C13
Deeping St Nicholas 23 D11
Deerness 56 F5
Deganwy 18 C7
Delabole 3 C8
Delchirach 49 E12
Delves 37 H10
Denbigh 18 D10
Denby Dale 27 E13
Denholm 36 B4
Denny 39 B13
Dent 31 F13
Denton
- Grt Manchester 27 F10
- Lincs 22 B7
Derby 22 B2
Dereham 24 D4
Dersingham 24 B1
Dervaig 42 C6
Desborough 22 G6
Desford 22 E3
Devil's Bridge 19 N7
Devizes 8 A5
Devonport 3 F12
Dewsbury 27 C13
Diabaig 46 E8
Dibden Purlieu 9 G9
Dickleborough 24 G6
Didcot 15 H14
Digby 29 J9
Dinas Mawddwy 19 J8
Dinas Powis 7 D10
Dingwall 48 C6
Dinnington 28 F4
Dinton 8 D5
Dippen 38 H5
Dirleton 41 E8
Diss 24 G6
Distington 30 B6
Ditchingham 24 F8
Ditchling 10 H4
Dittisham 4 H2
Ditton Priors 20 H7
Dobwalls 3 E10
Docking 24 B2
Dockray 31 B9
Doddinghurst 17 F10
Doddington
- Cambs 23 F12
- Northumb 41 K12
Dolanog 20 E1
Dolfor 20 H2
Dolgarrog 18 D7
Dolgellau 19 J7
Dollar 40 D2
Dolphinton 40 J4
Dolton 6 K4
Dolwyddelan 18 E7
Doncaster 28 D4
Donhead StAndrew 8 E4
Donington 23 B11
Donnington 21 E8
Dorchester
- Dorset 5 E10
- Oxon 15 G14
Dores 48 E7
Dorking 10 E2
Dornie 47 J8
Dornoch 53 K9
Dorridge 21 J12
Dorstone 14 B2
Douglas
- IoM 30 H3
- S Lanark 39 G13
Dounby 56 D2
Doune 45 J9
Dounreay 53 B11
Dove Holes 27 H11
Dover 11 E14
Doveridge 21 C12
Downham 23 G14
Downham Market 24 E1
Downton 8 E6
Drayton 24 D6
Dreghorn 39 G8
Drem 41 F8
Driffield 33 J12
Drigg 30 D6
Drimnin 42 C7
Droitwich Spa 21 K10
Dronfield 28 G2
Drongan 34 B5
Druid 18 F10
Drumbeg 52 E3
Drumgask 48 J7
Drumjohn 34 D6
Drummore 34 K2
Drumnadrochit 48 E6
Drymen 39 B9
Drynoch 47 H4
Duchally 52 G5
Duddington 23 E8
Dudley 21 G10
Duffield 22 A2
Dufftown 50 D2
Dukinfield 27 F10
Dullingham 25 K1
Dulnain Bridge 49 F10
Duloe 3 F10
Dulverton 4 A3
Dumbarton 39 C9
Dumfries 35 F10
Dunans 38 A5
Dunbar 41 F9
Dunbeath 53 F13
Dunblane 45 J9
Dunchurch 22 H3
Dundee 51 P2
Dundonald 39 G8
Dundrennan 35 J8
Dunecht 50 G6
Dunfermline 40 E4
Dungraggan 44 J7
Dunino 41 B8
Dunipace 39 B13
Dunkeld 45 E12
Dunlop 39 F9
Dunnet 53 B14
Dunning 45 H12
Dunnington 33 J8
Dunoon 38 C6
Dunragit 34 H2
Duns 41 H10
Dunsby 23 C10
Dunscore 35 E9
Dunsford 4 E2
Dunstable 16 C5
Dunster 7 G8
Dunston 21 E10
Dunsyre 40 J3
Dunure 34 B3
Dunvegan 46 G2
Dunwich 25 J9
Durham 37 J11
Durness 52 B6
Durrington 8 C6
Dursley 14 G6
Dyce 50 F7
Dykehead 51 L2
Dymchurch 11 G12
Dymock 14 C5
Dysart 40 D6
Dyserth 26 H1

E

Eaglescliffe 32 C6
Eaglesfield 35 F13
Eaglesham 39 E10
Eakring 28 H5
Ealing 10 B2
Earby 27 A10
Eardisley 14 B2
Earith 23 H12
Earls Barton 22 J7
Earl's Colne 25 N3
Earlsferry 41 C8
Earl Shilton 22 F3
Earl Soham 25 J7
Earlston 41 K8
Earsdon 37 F12
Easdale 42 G9
Easebourne 9 E14
Easington
- Durham 37 J13
- E Yorks 29 C12
Easington Colliery 37 J13
Easingwold 32 G7
East Bergholt 25 M5
East Boldre 9 H8
Eastbourne 10 K7
East Brent 7 F12
East Bridgford 22 A5
East Calder 40 G3
Eastchurch 11 B11
East Cowes 9 H10
East Cowton 32 D4
East Dean 10 K6
Easter Skeld 57 H4
Eastfield 33 F12
East Grinstead 10 F4
East Harling 24 G4
East Horsley 10 D1
East Ilsley 15 H14
East Kilbride 39 E11
East Leake 22 C4
Eastleigh 9 F9
East Linton 41 F8
East Looe 3 F10
East Markham 28 G6
Eastnor 14 C6
East Norton 22 E6
East Oakley 9 C10
Easton
- Dorset 5 F10
- N Nhants 23 E9
Easton-in-Gordano 14 J4
Eastry 11 D14
East Wemyss 40 D6
East Wittering 9 H13
East Witton 32 F3
Eastwood 28 K3
East Woodhay 9 A9
Eaton 22 C6
Eaton Socon 23 K10
Ebberston 33 F11
Ebbw Vale 7 A10
Ecclaw 41 G10
Ecclefechan 35 F12
Eccleshall 21 D9
Eccleston 26 A5
Echt 50 G6
Eckington
- Derbys 28 G3
- Worcs 15 B8
Edderton 53 K9
Edenbridge 10 E5
Edgmond 21 E8
Edinburgh 40 F5
Edington 8 B4
Edmundbyers 37 J9
Edwinstowe 28 H5
Edzell 51 L5
Egham 16 J5
Eglwyswrw 12 C5
Egremont 30 C6
Egton 33 D10
Eilean Iarmain 47 K7
Eisgean 55 F5
Elan Village 19 P9
Elgin 49 B13
Elgol 47 K5
Elham 11 E12
Elie 40 C7
Elishaw 36 D7
Elland 27 C12
Ellesmere 20 C5
Ellesmere Port 26 H4
Ellington 37 D11
Ellon 50 D8
Elmswell 25 J4
Elphin 52 G4
Elsdon 37 D8
Elsenham 17 C10
Elstead 9 C14
Elston 22 A6
Elvanfoot 35 B10
Elveden 24 H3
Elvington 33 K8
Elworth 27 J8
Ely 23 G14
Embleton 37 A11
Embo 53 J10
Empingham 23 E8
Emsworth 9 G12
Enderby 22 F4
Endon 21 A10
Enfield 17 F8
Enstone 15 D12
Enterkinfoot 35 C9
Epping 17 E9
Epsom 10 D3
Epworth 28 D6
Eriboll 52 C6
Errogie 48 F6
Errol 45 G14
Erskine 39 C9
Erskine Bridge 39 C9
Escrick 33 K8
Esher 10 C2
Esh Winning 37 J10
Eskdalemuir 35 D13
Eston 32 B7
Etchingham 11 G8
Eton 16 H4
Ettington 15 B11
Etwall 21 C13
Euxton 26 C6
Evanton 48 B7
Evercreech 8 D1
Everleigh 8 B7
Evershot 5 C9
Evesham 15 B9
Ewell 10 C3
Ewhurst 10 F1
Ewyas Harold 14 D2
Exbourne 3 A14
Exeter 4 D3
Exford 6 H7
Exminster 4 E3
Exmouth 4 F3
Exton 23 D8
Eyam 27 H13
Eye
- Pboro 23 E11
- Suff 25 H6
Eyemouth 41 G12
Eyethorne 11 E13
Eynsford 10 C6
Eynsham 15 F13

F

Faddiley 20 A6
Fairbourne 19 J6
Fairford 15 F10
Fairlie 38 E7
Fairlight 11 H9
Fakenham 24 B4
Fala 40 G7

Faldingworth 29 F9
Falkirk 39 B13
Falkland 40 C5
Falmer 10 J4
Falmouth 2 H6
Falstone 36 E6
Fareham 9 G10
Faringdon 15 G11
Farnborough
Hants 9 B13
W Berks 15 H13
Farndon 20 A5
Farnham 9 C13
Farnworth 27 E8
Farr 48 E7
Fasag 46 F9
Faslane 38 A7
Fauldhouse 40 G2
Faversham 11 C11
Fawley 9 G9
Fazeley 21 F13
Fearn 49 A9
Fearnan 45 E9
Feckenham 21 K11
Felixstowe 25 M8
Felton 37 C10
Feltwell 24 F2
Fenny Bentley 21 A12
Fenny Compton 15 A13
Fenny Stratford 16 B3
Fenwick 39 F9
Feock 2 H6
Feolin Ferry 43 M6
Ferndown 8 H5
Ferness 49 D10
Fernhurst 9 E14
Ferryhill 32 A4
Ferryside 12 F7
Fettercairn 51 K5
Filby 24 D9
Filey 33 F13
Fillongley 21 H13
Filton 14 J5
Fincham 24 E1
Finchingfield 17 B11
Finchley 16 F7
Findhorn 49 B11
Findochty 50 A3
Findon 10 J2
Finedon 23 H8
Finningley 28 E5
Finstown 56 E3
Fintry 39 B11
Fionnphort 42 F4
Fishbourne 9 H10
Fishguard 12 C3
Fishnish 42 D8
Fishtoft 23 A12
Flamborough 33 G14
Fleet 9 B13
Fleetwood 31 K9
Flimby 35 K11
Flint 26 H3
Flitwick 16 B5
Flodden 41 K12
Flookburgh 31 G9
Fochabers 50 B2
Foel 19 J10
Folkestone 11 F13
Folkingham 23 B9
Fontmell Magna 8 F3
Ford 43 H10
Forden 20 F3
Fordham 25 H1
Fordingbridge 8 F6
Fordyce 50 A4
Forest Row 10 F5
Forfar 51 M3
Formby 26 E3
Forres 49 C11
Forsinain 53 D11
Forsinard 53 D10
Fort Augustus 48 H4
Fort George
Highland 49 C8
Jersey 4 Jersey
Forth 40 H2
Forth Road Bridge 40 E4
Fortrie 50 C5
Fortrose 49 C8
Fortuneswell 5 F10
Fort William 44 B3
Fothergill 35 K11
Fotheringhay 23 F9
Foulden 41 H12
Foulsham 24 C5
Fountainhall 40 J7
Four Lanes 2 H4
Fovant 8 E5
Fowey 3 F9
Fownhope 14 C4
Foxdale 30 H2
Foyers 48 F6
Fraddon 2 F6
Framlingham 25 J7
Frampton on Severn 14 F6
Frant 10 F6
Fraserburgh 50 A8
Freckleton 26 C5
Freethorpe 24 E9
Fremington 6 H4
Frensham 9 C13
Freshwater 9 J8
Freshwater East 12 G4
Fressingfield 24 H7
Freswick 53 B15
Freuchie 40 C5
Friday Bridge 23 E13
Fridaythorpe 33 H10
Frimley 9 B13
Frinton-on-Sea 25 P7
Friockheim 51 M4
Frizington 30 C6
Frodsham 26 H6
Frome 8 C2
Frongoch 18 G9
Froxfield 15 K11
Fulbourn 23 K14
Fulford 33 K8
Fulwood 26 B6
Funzie 57 C7
Furnace 44 J2
Fyfield 17 E10
Fyvie 50 D6

G

Gaerwen 18 C4
Gaick Lodge 49 K8
Gailey 21 E10
Gainford 32 C3
Gainsborough 28 F7
Gairloch 46 D8
Gairlochy 44 A3
Galashiels 40 K7
Galgate 31 J10
Galmisdale 47 N4
Galmpton 4 H2
Galston 39 G10
Gamlingay 23 K11
Garbhallt 38 A5
Garboldisham 24 G5
Gardenstown 50 A7
Garelochhead 38 A7
Garforth 28 A3
Gargrave 32 J1
Gargunnock 39 A12
Garlieston 34 J5
Garmouth 50 A2
Garrow 45 E10
Garsdale Head 31 E13
Garstang 31 K10
Garston 26 G4
Garton-on-the-Wolds 33 H11
Garvald 41 F8
Garvard 43 J5
Garve 48 B4
Gatehouse of Fleet 34 H6
Gateshead 37 G11
Gatley 27 G9
Gatwick Airport 10 E3
Gawthwaite 31 F8
Gaydon 15 A12
Gayton 24 D2
Gaywood 24 C1
Gearraidh na h-Aibhne 55 D4
Geary 46 E2
Geddington 22 G7
Gedney 23 C13
Gedney Drove End 23 C13
Georgeham 6 H3
Gerrards Cross 16 G5
Gifford 41 G8
Giggleswick 31 H14
Gillingham
Dorset 5 A11
Medway 17 J12
Gilmerton 45 G10
Gilsland 36 G5
Gilwern 14 E1
Giosla 55 E3
Girton 23 J13
Girvan 34 D3
Gisburn 31 K14
Gladestry 14 A1
Glamis 51 N2
Glanaman 13 E10
Glanton 37 B9
Glasbury 13 C15
Glasgow 39 D10
Glasserton 34 K5
Glasson 31 J10
Glastonbury 7 H14
Glemsford 25 L3
Glenbarr 38 G1
Glenborrodale 42 B8
Glenbrittle 47 J4
Glencaple 35 G10
Glencarse 45 G14
Glencoe 44 D3
Glendoll Lodge 51 K1
Gleneagles 45 H11
Glenelg 47 K8
Glenfinnan 47 N9
Glenluce 34 H3
Glenmaye 30 G2
Glenmore Lodge 49 H10
Glenprosen Lodge 51 L1
Glenrothes 40 C5
Glenstriven 38 C5
Glentrool Village 34 F4
Glenwhilly 34 F3
Glinton 23 E10
Glossop 27 F11
Gloucester 14 E7
Glusburn 27 A11
Glutt Lodge 53 E11
Glyn Ceiriog 20 C3
Glyncorrwg 13 G12
Glynde 10 J5
Glyndyfrdwy 20 B2
Glyn Neath 13 F12
Gnosall 21 D9
Goathland 33 D10
Gobowen 20 C4
Godalming 9 C14
Godmanchester 23 H11
Godshill 9 J10
Godstone 10 E4
Goldhanger 25 Q4
Golspie 53 J10
Goodrich 14 E4
Goodwick 12 C3
Goole 28 B6
Goonhavern 2 F5
Gordon 41 J9
Gorebridge 40 G6
Gorey 5 Jersey
Goring 16 G1
Goring-by-Sea 10 J2
Gorleston-on-Sea 24 E10
Gorran Haven 3 H8
Gorseinon 13 G9
Gorslas 13 E9
Gosberton 23 B11
Gosfield 25 N2
Gosforth 30 D6
Gosport 9 H11
Goswick 41 J13
Gotham 22 C4
Goudhurst 11 F8
Gourdon 51 K7
Gourock 38 C7
Gowerton 13 G9
Grabhair 55 F5
Grain 11 B9
Grainthorpe 29 E12
Grampound 2 G7
Gramsdal 54 D5
Grangemouth 40 E2
Grange-over-Sands 31 G10
Grantham 23 B8
Grantown-on-Spey 49 F11
Grantshouse 41 G11
Grasby 29 D9
Grasmere 31 D9
Grassington 32 H2
Grateley 8 C7
Gravesend 17 H11
Grayrigg 31 E11
Grays 17 H11
Grayshott 9 D13
Great Ayton 32 C7
Great Baddow 17 E12
Great Barford 23 K10
Great Bentley 25 N6
Great Bridgeford 21 D9
Great Broughton 32 D7
Great Chesterford 17 A10
Great Clifton 30 B6
Great Dunmow 17 C11
Great Ellingham 24 F5
Great Gidding 23 G10
Greatham 32 B6
Great Harwood 27 B8
Great Horwood 16 B2
Great Malvern 14 B6
Great Massingham 24 C2
Great Missenden 16 E4
Great Oakley 25 N7
Great Sampford 17 B11
Great Shefford 15 J12
Great Shelford 23 K13
Great Somerford 15 H8
Great Staunton 23 H10
Great Torrington 6 K3
Great Wakering 17 G14
Great Waltham 17 D12
Great Witley 21 K8
Great Yarmouth 24 E10
Green Hammerton 32 J6
Greenhead 36 G5
Greenholm 39 G10
Greenlaw 41 J10
Greenloaning 45 J10
Greenock 38 C7
Greenodd 31 F9
Greenway 12 D4
Greenwich 10 B4
Gretna 36 G2
Gretna Green 36 G2
Gretton 23 F8
Greystoke 31 A10
Grimsby 29 D11
Gritley 56 F5
Grizebeck 31 F8
Groby 22 E4
Grove 15 G13
Grundisburgh 25 L7
Gualachulain 44 E3
Guard Bridge 40 B7
Guestling Green 11 H9
Guildford 10 E1
Guildtown 45 F13
Guilsfield 20 E3
Guisborough 33 C8
Guiseley 27 A12
Gullane 40 E7
Gunnerside 32 E1
Gunnislake 3 D12
Gunnista 57 H6
Gutcher 57 B6
Gwalchmai 18 C3
Gwaun-Cae-Gurwen 13 E10
Gwbert 12 B5
Gweek 2 J4
Gwennap 2 H5
Gwyddelwern 18 F10
Gwytherin 18 D8
Gyre 56 F3

H

Hackney 10 A4
Hackthorpe 31 B11
Haddenham
Bucks 16 E2
Cambs 23 H13
Haddington 41 F8
Haddiscoe 24 F9
Hadleigh
Essex 17 G13
Suff. 25 L5
Hadlow 10 E7
Hadnall 20 D6
Hagworthingham 29 H12
Hailsham 10 J6
Hainton 29 F10
Halberton 4 B4
Halesowen 21 H10
Halesworth 24 H8
Halford 15 B11
Halifax 27 C11
Halkirk 53 C13
Halland 10 H6
Hallow 14 A7
Hallworthy 3 C9
Halstead 25 M3
Halton 31 H11
Haltwhistle 36 G6
Halwill Junction 3 B12
Hambledon 9 F11
Hamble-le-Rice 9 G9
Hambleton
Lancs 26 A4
N Yorks 28 A4
Hamerton 23 H10
Hamilton 39 E12
Hammersmith & Fulham 10 B3
Hamnavoe
Shetland 57 E6
Shetland 57 J4
Hampstead Norreys 15 J14
Hampton in Arden 21 H13
Hamstreet 11 F11
Handcross 10 G3
Hannington 9 B10
Harbury 22 J2
Harby 22 B6
Hardingstone 22 K6
Harewood 27 A14
Haringey 10 A4
Harlech 18 G5
Harleston 24 G7
Harlow 17 E9
Haroldswick 57 A7
Harpenden 16 D6
Harrietfield 45 F11
Harrietsham 11 D9
Harrington 30 B5
Harris 47 M3
Harrogate 32 J4
Harrold 23 K8
Harrow 16 G6
Harston 23 K13
Hartburn 37 E9
Hartest 25 K3
Hartfield 10 F5
Harthill 40 G2
Hartington 27 J12
Hartland 6 J1
Hartlebury 21 J9
Hartlepool 32 A7
Hartley
Kent 17 J11
Northumb 37 F12
Hartley Wintney 9 B12
Hartpury 14 D6
Hartshill 22 F2
Harvington 15 B9
Harwell 15 H13
Harwich 25 M7
Harworth 28 E5
Haselbury Plucknett 5 C8

Haslemere.....9 D13
Haslingden.....27 C8
Hassocks.....10 H4
Hastigrow.....53 C14
Hastings.....11 J9
Haswell.....37 J12
Hatch Beauchamp....4 B7
Hatfield
  Herts.....16 E7
  S Yorks.....28 D5
Hatfield Heath....17 D10
Hatfield Peverel....17 D13
Hatherleigh.....3 A13
Hathersage.....27 G13
Hatton
  Aberds.....50 D9
  Derbys.....21 C13
Haughley.....25 J5
Haugh of Urr.....35 G8
Haughton.....21 D9
Havant.....9 G12
Haverfordwest.....12 E3
Haverhill.....17 A11
Haverigg.....30 F7
Havering.....17 G10
Hawarden.....26 J4
Hawes.....31 E14
Hawick.....36 B4
Hawkchurch.....4 D7
Hawkesbury Upton..14 H6
Hawkhurst.....11 G8
Hawkinge.....11 F13
Hawkshead.....31 E9
Hawnby.....32 E7
Hawsker.....33 D11
Haxby.....33 J8
Haxey.....28 D6
Haydon Bridge.....36 G7
Hayfield.....27 G11
Hayle.....2 H3
Hay-on-Wye.....14 B1
Hayton
  Cumb.....36 H4
  E Yorks.....33 K10
Haywards Heath....10 G4
Hazel Grove.....27 G10
Hazlemere.....16 F4
Heacham.....24 B1
Headcorn.....11 E9
Headley.....9 D13
Heanor.....22 A3
Heath End.....9 A10
Heathfield.....10 H6
Heathrow Airport....16 H5
Hebburn.....37 G12
Hebden Bridge.....27 C10
Heckington.....23 A10
Hedge End.....9 F10
Hednesford.....21 E11
Hedon.....29 B10
Heighington.....32 B4
Heilam.....52 B6
Helensburgh.....39 B8
Hellifield.....31 J14
Helmsdale.....53 G12
Helmsley.....33 F8
Helperby.....32 G6
Helpringham.....23 A10
Helsby.....26 H5
Helston.....2 J4
Hemel Hempstead..16 E5
Hemingbrough.....28 A5
Hempnall.....24 F7
Hempton.....24 C4
Hemsby.....24 D9
Hemsworth.....28 C3
Hemyock.....4 B5
Henfield.....10 H3
Hengoed.....7 B10
Henley-in-Arden..21 K12
Henley-on-Thames..16 G2
Henllan.....18 D10
Henlow.....16 B6
Henstridge.....5 B11
Herbrandston.....12 F2

Hereford.....14 C4
Heriot.....40 H7
Hermitage.....15 J14
Herne Bay.....11 C12
Herstmonceux.....10 H7
Herston.....56 G4
Hertford.....17 D8
Hessle.....29 B9
Heswall.....26 G3
Hethersett.....24 E6
Hetton-le-Hole....37 J12
Hexham.....37 G8
Heybridge.....17 E13
Heysham.....31 H10
Heytesbury.....8 C4
Heywood.....27 D9
Hibaldstow.....29 D8
Higham.....17 H12
Higham Ferrers....23 J8
High Bentham.....31 G12
High Bickington....6 K4
Highbridge.....7 G12
Highclere.....9 B9
High Ercall.....20 E7
High Hesket.....36 J3
High Legh.....27 G8
Highley.....21 H8
Hightae.....35 F11
Highworth.....15 G11
High Wycombe....16 F3
Hilborough.....24 E3
Hildenborough....10 E6
Hilgay.....24 F1
Hillingdon.....16 G5
Hillington.....24 C2
Hillswick.....57 E3
Hilmarton.....15 J9
Hilton.....21 C13
Hinckley.....22 F3
Hinderwell.....33 C10
Hindhead.....9 D13
Hindley.....26 E7
Hindon.....8 D4
Hingham.....24 E5
Hinstock.....20 D8
Hirwaun.....13 F13
Histon.....23 J13
Hitchin.....16 B6
Hockley.....17 F13
Hockliffe.....16 C4
Hoddesdon.....17 E8
Hodnet.....20 D7
Hoff.....31 C12
Holbeach.....23 C12
Holbeach Drove....23 D12
Holbrook.....25 M6
Holford.....7 G10
Holkham.....24 A3
Holland-on-Sea....25 P7
Hollandstoun.....56 A7
Hollym.....29 B12
Holme-on-Spalding-
  moor.....28 A7
Holmer.....14 B4
Holmes Chapel.....27 J8
Holmfirth.....27 E12
Holsworthy.....3 A11
Holt
  Norf.....24 B5
  Wrex.....20 A5
Holyhead.....18 B2
Holywell.....26 H2
Honington.....23 A8
Honiton.....4 D5
Hook.....9 B12
Hook Norton.....15 C12
Hope.....26 K4
Hopeman.....49 A12
Hope under
  Dinmore.....14 A4
Horam.....10 H6
Horden.....37 J13
Horley.....10 E3
Horncastle.....29 H11
Horndean.....9 F12
Horningsham.....8 C3
Hornsea.....33 K13
Horrabridge.....3 E13
Horringer.....25 J3

Horsey.....24 C9
Horsford.....24 D6
Horsforth.....27 B13
Horsham.....10 F2
Horsham St Faith....24 D7
Horsted Keynes.....10 G4
Horton
  Som.....4 B7
  W Nhants.....22 K7
Horton in
  Ribblesdale.....31 G14
Horwich.....26 D7
Houghton-le-
  Spring.....37 H12
Houghton Regis....16 C5
Hounslow.....10 B2
Hove.....10 J3
Hoveton.....24 D7
Hovingham.....33 G8
Howden.....28 B6
Howpasley.....36 C2
Hoxne.....24 H6
Hoylake.....26 G3
Hucknall.....28 K4
Huddersfield.....27 D12
Hugh Town.....2 C3
Hulland Ward.....21 B13
Hullavington.....14 H7
Hullbridge.....17 F13
Hulme End.....27 K12
Humber Bridge....29 B9
Humberston.....29 D11
Humshaugh.....37 F8
Hunmanby.....33 G12
Hunstanton.....24 A1
Huntford.....36 C5
Huntingdon.....23 H11
Huntley.....14 E6
Huntly.....50 C4
Hurlford.....39 G9
Hurliness.....56 H2
Hurn.....8 H6
Hursley.....9 E9
Hurstbourne Tarrant..9 B8
Hurstpierpoint.....10 H3
Hurworth-on-Tees..32 C5
Husbands Bosworth..22 G5
Husinish.....55 F2
Huttoft.....29 G14
Hutton.....26 C5
Hutton Cranswick..33 J12
Hutton-le-Hole....33 E9
Hutton Rudby.....32 D6
Huyton.....26 F5
Hyde.....27 F10
Hynish.....42 E1
Hythe
  Hants.....9 G9
  Kent.....11 F12

I

Ibsey.....8 G6
Ibstock.....22 D2
Icklingham.....25 H2
Idmiston.....8 D7
Ilchester.....5 A9
Ilderton.....37 A9
Ilfracombe.....6 G4
Ilkeston.....22 A3
Ilkley.....32 K3
Illogan.....2 G4
Ilminster.....4 B7
Immingham.....29 C10
Inchnadamph.....52 F4
Inchture.....45 F14
Ingatestone.....17 F11
Ingleton.....31 G12
Ingoldmells.....29 H14
Ingram.....37 B9
Ingrave.....17 F11
Inkberrow.....15 A9
Innellan.....38 C6
Innerleithen.....40 K6
Innermessan.....34 G2
Insch.....50 E5

Instow.....6 J3
Inver.....53 K10
Inveran.....52 J7
Inveraray.....44 J2
Inverarity.....51 N3
Inverbervie.....51 K7
Invergarry.....48 H4
Invergordon.....49 B8
Invergowrie.....51 P2
Inverie.....47 L7
Inverinate.....47 J9
Inverkeilor.....51 M5
Inverkeithing.....40 E4
Inverkirkaig.....52 F2
Inverlochlarig.....44 H6
Invermoriston.....48 G5
Inverness.....48 D7
Inversnaid.....44 J5
Inverurie.....50 E6
Ipswich.....25 L6
Irchester.....23 J8
Irlam.....27 F8
Ironbridge.....20 F7
Irthlingborough....23 H8
Irvine.....39 G8
Isbister.....57 C4
Isleham.....25 H1
Isle of Whithorn..34 K5
Islington.....10 A4
Islip.....15 E14
Ivinghoe.....16 D4
Ivybridge.....3 F14
Iwerne Minster.....8 F3
Ixworth.....25 H4

J

Jamestown.....39 B8
Jarrow.....37 G12
Jaywick.....25 P6
Jedburgh.....36 A5
John o' Groats.....53 A15
Johnshaven.....51 L7
Johnston.....12 F3
Johnstone.....39 D9

K

Kames.....38 C4
Kea.....2 G5
Kearvaig.....52 A4
Kedington.....17 A11
Keelby.....29 C10
Keele.....21 B9
Kegworth.....22 C3
Keighley.....27 A11
Keillmore.....38 B1
Keiss.....53 B15
Keith.....50 B3
Keld.....31 D14
Kellas.....49 C12
Kelsale.....25 J8
Kelsall.....26 J6
Kelso.....41 K10
Keltneyburn.....45 E9
Kelty.....40 D4
Kelvedon.....17 D13
Kelynack.....2 J1
Kemble.....15 G9
Kemnay.....50 F6
Kempsey.....14 B7
Kempston.....16 A5
Kemsing.....10 D6
Kendal.....31 E11
Kenilworth.....22 H1
Kenmore.....45 E9
Kennacraig.....38 D3
Kennethmont.....50 E4
Kennford.....4 E3
Kenninghall.....24 G5
Kennington.....15 F14
Kensington &
  Chelsea.....10 B3
Kentford.....25 J2
Kentisbeare.....4 C4
Kerry.....20 H2

Kerrysdale.....46 D8
Kershopefoot.....36 E3
Kesgrave.....25 L7
Kessingland.....24 G10
Keswick.....31 B8
Kettering.....22 H7
Kettletoft.....56 C6
Kettlewell.....32 G1
Ketton.....23 E8
Kew Bridge.....10 B3
Kexby.....28 F7
Keyingham.....29 B11
Keymer.....10 H4
Keynsham.....14 K5
Keysoe.....23 J9
Keyworth.....22 B5
Kibworth
  Beauchamp.....22 F5
Kidderminster.....21 J9
Kidlington.....15 E14
Kidsgrove.....21 A9
Kidstones.....32 F1
Kidwelly.....12 F8
Kielder.....36 D5
Kilberry.....38 D2
Kilbirnie.....39 E8
Kilcadzow.....39 F13
Kilchattan.....38 E6
Kilchenzie.....38 H1
Kilchiaran.....43 M4
Kilchoan.....42 B6
Kilchrenan.....44 G2
Kilcreggan.....38 B7
Kildonan.....53 F11
Kilfinan.....38 C4
Kilham.....33 H12
Kilkhampton.....3 A10
Killamarsh.....28 F3
Killean.....38 F1
Killearn.....39 B10
Killin.....44 F7
Killinghall.....32 J4
Kilmacolm.....39 D8
Kilmaluag.....46 D4
Kilmany.....40 A6
Kilmarnock.....39 G9
Kilmartin.....38 A3
Kilmaurs.....39 F9
Kilmelford.....42 G10
Kilmore.....42 F10
Kilmory
  Argyll.....38 C2
  Highland.....42 A7
  Highland.....47 L3
Kilmuir.....49 A8
Kilninver.....42 F10
Kilnsea.....29 C13
Kilrenny.....41 C8
Kilsby.....22 H4
Kilsyth.....39 C12
Kilwinning.....38 F7
Kimbolton.....23 J9
Kimpton.....16 D6
Kinbrace.....53 F10
Kinbuck.....45 J10
Kincardine
  Fife.....40 E2
  Highland.....52 K8
Kincardine Bridge..40 E2
Kincraig.....49 H9
Kineton.....15 A12
Kingarth.....38 E5
Kinghorn.....40 E5
Kingsbarns.....41 B8
Kingsbridge.....4 J1
Kingsbury.....21 G13
Kingsclere.....9 B10
King's Cliffe.....23 F9
Kingsdown.....11 E14
Kingskerswell.....4 G2
Kingsland.....20 K5
Kings Langley.....16 E5
Kingsley
  Hants.....9 D12
  Staffs.....21 B11
King's Lynn.....24 D1
King's Somborne..9 D8
Kingsteignton.....4 F2
King's Thorn.....14 C4

Kingston
Devon.............3 G14
London...........10 C2
Kingston Bagpuize .15 G13
Kingston upon Hull . 29 B9
Kingswear...........4 J2
Kingswood.........14 J5
King's Worthy......9 D10
Kington.............14 A2
Kingussie.........49 H8
Kinloch
Highland......47 M4
Highland......52 E5
Kinlochbervie......52 C4
Kinlochewe........47 N9
Kinlochmoidart....42 A9
Kinlochleven......44 C3
Kinloch Rannoch...45 D8
Kinloss..........49 B11
Kinmel Bay.......18 C9
Kinross..........40 C4
Kintessack.......49 C10
Kintore..........50 F6
Kinuachdrachd....43 J9
Kinver...........21 H9
Kippax...........28 A3
Kippen...........39 A11
Kirkabister......57 J5
Kirkbean.........35 H10
Kirkbride........35 H13
Kirkburton.......27 D12
Kirkby...........26 F5
Kirkby-in-Ashfield . 28 J4
Kirkby-in-Furness . 31 F8
Kirkby Lonsdale . 31 G12
Kirkby Malzeard...32 G4
Kirkbymoorside...33 F8
Kirkby Stephen...31 D13
Kirkby Thore.....31 B12
Kirkcaldy........40 D5
Kirkcolm.........34 G1
Kirkconnel.......35 B8
Kirkcowan........34 G4
Kirkcudbright....34 H8
Kirkham..........26 B5
Kirkinner........34 H5
Kirkintilloch....39 C11
Kirkland.........35 D9
Kirkliston.......40 F4
Kirkmichael
Perth.........45 C12
S Ayrs........34 C4
Kirk Michael.....30 F3
Kirknewton......41 K12
Kirkoswald
Cumb..........36 J4
S Ayrs........34 C3
Kirkpatrick Durham . 35 F8
Kirkpatrick Fleming 35 F13
Kirkton of Glenisla .45 C14
Kirkton of Largo...40 C7
Kirkwall.........56 E4
Kirkwhelpington..37 E9
Kirriemuir.......51 M2
Kirtling.........25 K1
Kirtlington......15 D14
Kirton...........23 B11
Kirton in Lindsey.29 E8
Knaresborough....32 J5
Knayton..........32 F6
Knebworth........16 D7
Knighton.........20 J3
Knott End-on-Sea..31 K9
Knottingley......28 B3
Knowle...........21 J12
Knutsford........27 H8
Kyleakin.........47 J7
Kyle of Lochalsh..47 J7
Kylerhea.........47 J7
Kylestrome.......52 E4

L
Laceby..........29 D11
Lacock..........15 K8
Ladock...........2 G6
Ladybank.........40 B6

Lagg
Argyll.........43 L7
N Ayrs.........38 H4
Laggan
Highland......48 J4
Highland......48 J7
Moray.........50 D2
Laide...........46 B9
Lairg...........52 H7
Lakenheath.......24 G2
Lamberhurst......10 F7
Lambeth.........10 B4
Lambley.........36 H5
Lambourn........15 J12
Lamlash.........38 G5
Lampeter........13 B9
Lanark..........39 F13
Lancaster.......31 H10
Lanchester......37 J10
Lancing.........10 J2
Landkey..........6 J4
Landrake.........3 F11
Langford Budville..7 J10
Langham.........22 D7
Langholm........36 E2
Langport.........7 J13
Langsett........27 E13
Langtoft
E Yorks.......33 H12
Lincs.........23 D10
Langton Matravers..8 K4
Langtree.........6 K3
Langwathby......31 H13
Langwell.........52 H8
Lanivet..........3 E8
Lapford..........4 C1
Larbert........39 B13
Largs...........38 E7
Larkhall........39 E12
Larkhill.........8 C6
Lasswade........40 G6
Latchingdon......17 E13
Latheron........53 E14
Lauder..........41 J8
Laugharne.......12 E6
Launceston.......3 C11
Laurencekirk....51 K6
Laurieston......34 G7
Lavendon........23 K8
Lavenham........25 L4
Lawers..........45 F8
Laxey...........30 G4
Laxfield........25 H7
Laxford Bridge...52 D4
Laxton..........28 H6
Layer de la Haye..25 P4
Lazonby.........36 J4
Lea.............28 F7
Leadburn........40 H5
Leadenham.......29 J8
Leaden Roding...17 D11
Leadgate........37 H10
Leadhills.......35 B9
Leasingham......29 K9
Leatherhead.....10 D2
Lechlade-on-
Thames.......15 G11
Ledbury.........14 C6
Ledmore.........52 G4
Leeds...........28 B13
Leedstown.......2 H3
Leek............27 K10
Leeming Bar.....32 E4
Lee-on-the-Solent .9 H10
Legbourne......29 F12
Leicester.......22 E4
Leigh
Grt Manchester..26 E7
Worcs.........14 A6
Leighton Buzzard..16 C4
Leintwardine....20 J5
Leiston.........25 J9
Leith...........40 F5
Leitholm........41 J10
Lelant...........2 H3
Lendalfoot......34 D2
Lenham..........11 D10
Lennoxtown......39 C11
Leominster......14 A3

Lephin..........46 G1
Le Planel........4 Guern
Lerwick.........57 H5
Lesbury.........37 B11
Leslie..........40 C5
Lesmahagow.....39 F13
Leswalt.........34 G1
Letchworth......16 B7
Lettan..........56 B7
Letterston......12 D3
Lettoch........49 E12
Leuchars........40 A7
Leumrabhagh.....55 F5
Leven
E Yorks.......33 K13
Fife..........40 C6
Leverburgh / An t-
Ob............55 J2
Lewes...........10 J5
Lewisham........10 B4
Lewiston........48 F6
Leyburn.........32 E3
Leyland.........26 C6
Leysdown-on-Sea..11 C11
Lhanbryde.......49 B13
Liatrie.........48 E3
Lichfield.......21 F12
Lidgate.........25 K2
Lifton..........3 C11
Lilleshall......21 E8
Lincoln.........29 G8
Lindale.........31 F10
Lingfield.......10 E4
Linkinhorne......3 D11
Linksness.......56 F2
Linlithgow......40 F2
Linslade........16 C4
Linton..........17 A10
Liphook..........9 E13
Liskeard.........3 E10
Liss............9 E12
Litcham.........24 D3
Litherland......26 F4
Littleborough...27 D10
Littlehampton...10 J1
Littlemill......49 C10
Littleport......23 G14
Little Shelford..23 K13
Littlestone-on-Sea 11 G11
Little Stukeley..23 H11
Little Walsingham..24 B4
Littleton.......26 G4
Liverpool.......26 G5
Liverpool Airport..26 G5
Livingston......40 G3
Lizard...........2 K4
Llanaber........19 J5
Llanaelhaiarn...18 F3
Llanafan-fawr...19 Q9
Llanarmon Dyffryn
Ceiriog......20 C2
Llanarth........19 Q4
Llanarthne......13 E9
Llanbadarn Fynydd..20 J2
Llanbedr........18 H5
Llanbedrog......18 G3
Llanberis.......18 E5
Llanbister......20 J2
Llanbrynmair....19 K9
Llanddewi-Brefi..19 Q6
Llanddulas......18 C8
Llandeilo.......13 D10
Llandinam......19 M10
Llandissilio....12 D5
Llandogo........14 F4
Llandovery......13 C11
Llandrillo......18 G10
Llandrindod Wells .19 P10
Llandudno.......18 B7
Llandybie.......13 E10
Llandyfriog.....12 B7
Llandygwydd.....12 B6
Llandyrnog......26 J2
Llandysul.......12 B8
Llanelidan......20 B1
Llanelli........13 F9
Llanelltyd......19 J7
Llanenddwyn.....18 H5

Llanerchymedd.....18 B4
Llanerfyl........19 K10
Llanfaethlu......18 B3
Llanfair Caereinion .20 F2
Llanfairfechan...18 C6
Llanfairpwllgwngyll .18 C5
Llanfair Talhaiarn..18 C9
Llanfechain......20 E2
Llanfechell......18 B3
Llan Ffestiniog..18 F7
Llanfihangel-ar-arth 13 C8
Llanfrynach.....13 D14
Llanfyllin......20 E2
Llangadfan......19 J10
Llangadog......13 D11
Llangammarch
Wells........13 B13
Llangefni......18 C4
Llangeitho......19 Q6
Llangelynin.....19 K5
Llangennech.....13 F9
Llangernyw......18 D8
Llanglydwen....12 D5
Llangoed.......18 C6
Llangollen.....20 B3
Llangorse......13 D15
Llangranog......12 A7
Llangunllo......20 J3
Llangurig......19 N9
Llangwm........14 F3
Llangybi.......19 Q6
Llangynidr.....13 E15
Llangynog......18 H10
Llanharan.......7 C9
Llanidloes......19 M9
Llanilar.......19 N6
Llanllyfni......18 E4
Llannor........18 G3
Llanon.........19 P5
Llanpumsaint....12 D8
Llanrhaeadr-ym-
Mochnant.....20 D2
Llanrhian......12 C2
Llanrhidian....13 G8
Llanrhystyd.....19 N5
Llanrug........18 D5
Llanrwst.......18 D7
Llansannan.....18 D9
Llansawel......13 C10
Llanstephan.....12 E7
Llanthony......14 D1
Llantrisant.....7 C9
Llantwit-Major..13 K13
Llanuwchllyn...18 G8
Llanvihangel
Crucorney....14 D2
Llanwddyn......19 J10
Llanwenog......13 B8
Llanwrda.......13 C11
Llanwrtyd Wells .13 B12
Llanybydder....13 B9
Llanymynech....20 D3
Llanystumdwy...18 G4
Lledrod........19 N6
Llithfaen......18 F3
Llwyngwril.....19 J6
Llyswen........13 C15
Loanhead.......40 G5
Lochailort.....47 N7
Lochaline......42 D8
Lochans........34 H1
Locharbriggs...35 E10
Loch Baghasdail /
Lochboisdale..54 H4
Lochboisdale / Loch
Baghasdail...54 H4
Lochbuie.......42 F8
Loch Choire Lodge .52 E8
Lochdon........42 E9
Lochearnhead...44 G7
Loch Euphoirt...54 C5
Lochgair.......38 A4
Lochgelly......40 D4
Lochgilphead...38 B3
Lochgoilhead...44 J4
Lochinver......52 F2

Lochmaben......35 E11
Lochmaddy / Loch nam
Madadh......54 C6
Loch nam Madadh /
Lochmaddy...54 C6
Lochranza......38 E4
Loch Sgioport..54 F5
Lochwinnoch....39 D8
Lockerbie......35 E12
Lockton........33 E10
Loddiswell......4 J1
Loddon.........24 F8
Loftus.........33 C9
Logan..........34 A7
London.........10 B4
London Colney..16 E6
Long Ashton....14 K4
Long Bennington..22 A7
Longbenton.....37 G11
Longbridge Deverill . 8 C3
Long Clawson...22 C6
Long Compton...15 C11
Long Crendon...16 E1
Longdon........14 C7
Long Eaton.....22 B3
Longford.......14 D7
Longforgan.....51 P2
Longformacus...41 H10
Longframlington . 37 C10
Longhope.......56 G3
Longhorsley....37 D10
Longhoughton...37 B11
Long Itchington . 22 J3
Long Melford...25 L3
Longnor........27 J11
Long Preston...31 J14
Longridge......26 B7
Longside.......50 C9
Long Stratton..24 F6
Long Sutton...23 C13
Longtown
Cumb.........36 G2
Hereford.....14 D2
Loose..........11 D8
Lossiemouth....49 A13
Lostock Gralam..26 H8
Lostwithiel......3 F8
Loth...........56 C6
Loughborough...22 C4
Loughor........13 G9
Loughton.......17 F9
Louth..........29 F12
Lowdham........22 A5
Lower Beeding..10 G3
Lower Killeyan..43 P4
Lower Langford...7 F13
Lower Mayland..17 E14
Lower Shiplake..16 H2
Lowestoft......24 F10
Lowick.........41 J13
Loxwood........10 F1
Lubcroy........52 H5
Lucker.........41 K14
Ludborough....29 E11
Ludford........29 F10
Ludgershall.....8 B7
Ludgvan.........2 H2
Ludham.........24 D8
Ludlow.........20 J6
Lugton.........39 E9
Lugwardine.....14 B4
Lumphanan.....50 G4
Lumsden........50 E3
Luss...........39 A8
Lusta..........46 F2
Luton..........16 C5
Lutterworth....22 G4
Lutton.........23 G10
Lybster........53 E14
Lydd...........11 H11
Lydd on Sea....11 H11
Lydford.........3 C13
Lydham.........20 G4
Lydney.........14 F5
Lyme Regis......4 D7
Lyminge........11 E12

Lymington ... 9 H8
Lymm ... 26 G7
Lympne ... 11 F12
Lympstone ... 4 E3
Lyndhurst ... 8 G7
Lyneham ... 15 J9
Lyness ... 56 G3
Lynmouth ... 6 G6
Lynton ... 6 G6
Lytchett Minster ... 8 H4
Lytham St Anne's ... 26 C4
Lythe ... 33 C10

M
Mablethorpe ... 29 F13
Macclesfield ... 27 H10
Macduff ... 50 A5
Machen ... 7 C11
Machrihanish ... 38 H1
Machynlleth ... 19 K7
Macmerry ... 40 F7
Madeley ... 21 B8
Madley ... 14 C3
Maentwrog ... 18 G6
Maesteg ... 13 H12
Maghull ... 26 E4
Magor ... 14 H3
Maiden Bradley ... 8 D3
Maidenhead ... 16 H3
Maiden Newton ... 5 D9
Maidstone ... 11 D8
Maldon ... 17 E13
Malham ... 31 H14
Mallaig ... 47 M6
Mallwyd ... 19 J8
Malmesbury ... 15 H8
Malpas ... 20 B6
Maltby ... 28 E4
Maltby le Marsh ... 29 F13
Malton ... 33 G9
Manafon ... 20 F2
Manby ... 29 F13
Manchester ... 27 F9
Manchester Airport . 27 G9
Manea ... 23 G13
Mangotsfield ... 14 J5
Manningtree ... 25 M6
Manorbier ... 12 G4
Mansfield ... 28 H4
Mansfield
Woodhouse ... 28 H4
Manton ... 22 E7
Marazion ... 2 J3
Marbhig ... 55 F6
March ... 23 F13
Marden
  Hereford ... 14 B4
  Kent ... 11 E8
Mareham le Fen ... 29 H11
Maresfield ... 10 G5
Marfleet ... 29 B10
Margam ... 13 H11
Margate ... 11 C14
Marham ... 24 D2
Market Bosworth ... 22 E3
Market Deeping ... 23 D10
Market Drayton ... 20 C7
Market Harborough . 22 G6
Market Lavington ... 8 B5
Market Rasen ... 29 F10
Market Warsop ... 28 H4
Market Weighton ... 33 K10
Markfield ... 22 D3
Markinch ... 40 C6
Marks Tey ... 25 N4
Markyate ... 16 D5
Marlborough
  Devon ... 4 K1
  Wilts ... 15 K10
Marlow ... 16 G3
Marnhull ... 5 B11
Marple ... 27 G10
Marshchapel ... 29 E12
Marshfield ... 14 J6

Marske-by-the-Sea . 33 B8
Marston Magna ... 5 A9
Martham ... 24 D9
Martin ... 8 F5
Martley ... 21 K8
Martock ... 5 B8
Marton ... 28 F7
Marykirk ... 51 L5
Marypark ... 49 E12
Maryport ... 35 K11
Mary Tavy ... 3 D13
Marywell
  Aberds ... 51 H4
  Angus ... 51 N5
Masham ... 32 F4
Mathry ... 12 C2
Matlock ... 28 H1
Mattishall ... 24 D5
Mauchline ... 39 H9
Maud ... 50 C8
Maughold ... 30 F4
Mawgan ... 2 J5
Mawnan ... 2 J5
Maxwellheugh ... 41 K10
Maybole ... 34 C4
Mayfield
  E Sus ... 10 G6
  Staffs ... 21 B12
Mealabost ... 55 D6
Mealsgate ... 35 J13
Measham ... 22 D2
Medstead ... 9 D11
Meidrim ... 12 E6
Meifod ... 20 E2
Meigle ... 51 N1
Melbourn ... 17 A8
Melbourne ... 22 C2
Melgarve ... 48 J5
Melksham ... 8 A4
Mellon Charles ... 46 B8
Mellor ... 26 B7
Melmerby ... 36 K5
Melrose ... 41 K8
Melsonby ... 32 D3
Meltham ... 27 D12
Melton ... 25 K7
Melton Constable ... 24 B5
Melton Mowbray ... 22 D6
Melvaig ... 46 C7
Melvich ... 53 B10
Menai Bridge ... 18 C5
Mendlesham ... 25 J6
Mennock ... 35 C9
Menston ... 27 A12
Menstrie ... 39 A13
Meonstoke ... 9 F11
Meopham ... 17 J11
Mere ... 8 D3
Mere Brow ... 26 D5
Meriden ... 21 H13
Merriott ... 5 B8
Merthyr Tydfil ... 13 F14
Merton ... 10 C3
Meshaw ... 6 K6
Messingham ... 28 D7
Metfield ... 24 G7
Metheringham ... 29 H9
Methil ... 40 C6
Methlick ... 50 D7
Methven ... 45 G12
Methwold ... 24 F2
Mevagissey ... 3 G8
Mexborough ... 28 D3
Mey ... 53 A14
Micheldever ... 9 D10
Michelmersh ... 9 E8
Mickleover ... 22 B2
Mickleton
  Durham ... 32 B1
  Glos ... 15 B10
Midbea ... 56 B4
Middle Barton ... 15 D13
Middleham ... 32 F3
Middlemarsh ... 5 C10
Middlesbrough ... 32 B7
Middleton
  Argyll ... 42 D1
  Grt Manchester . 27 E9
  Norf ... 24 D1

Middleton Cheney .. 15 B14
Middleton-in-
  Teesdale ... 32 B1
Middleton-on-Sea .. 9 H14
Middleton on the
  Wolds ... 33 K11
Middlewich ... 26 J8
Middlezoy ... 7 H12
Midhurst ... 9 E13
Mid Lavant ... 9 G13
Midsomer Norton .. 8 B1
Mid Yell ... 57 C6
Milborne Port ... 5 B10
Mildenhall ... 24 H2
Milford ... 9 C14
Milford Haven ... 12 F2
Milford on Sea ... 8 H7
Millbrook ... 3 F12
Millom ... 30 F7
Millport ... 38 E6
Milnathort ... 40 C4
Milngavie ... 39 C10
Milnthorpe ... 31 F11
Milovaig ... 46 F1
Milton ... 48 C4
Milton Abbot ... 3 D11
Milton Keynes ... 16 B3
Milverton ... 7 J10
Minchinhampton ... 14 G7
Minehead ... 7 G8
Minera ... 20 A3
Minety ... 15 H9
Minnigaff ... 34 G5
Minster
  Kent ... 11 B10
  Kent ... 11 C14
Minsterley ... 20 F4
Mintlaw ... 50 C9
Mirfield ... 27 D13
Misterton
  Notts ... 28 E6
  Som ... 5 C8
Mistley ... 25 M6
Mitcheldean ... 14 E5
Mitchel Troy ... 14 F3
Modbury ... 3 F14
Moelfre ... 18 B5
Moffat ... 35 C11
Mold ... 26 J3
Monar Lodge ... 48 D3
Moniaive ... 35 D8
Monifieth ... 51 P4
Monikie ... 51 N4
Monkland ... 14 A3
Monkokehampton . 3 A13
Monkton ... 39 H8
Monmouth ... 14 E4
Montacute ... 5 B8
Montgomery ... 20 G3
Montrose ... 51 M6
Monymusk ... 50 F5
Morar ... 47 M6
Morchard Bishop ... 4 C1
Mordiford ... 14 C4
Morebattle ... 36 A6
Morecambe ... 31 H10
Moretonhampstead .. 4 E1
Moreton-in-Marsh . 15 C11
Morley ... 27 C13
Morpeth ... 37 E11
Mortehoe ... 6 G3
Mortimer's Cross ... 20 K5
Morwenstow ... 6 K1
Mossley ... 27 E10
Mostyn ... 26 H2
Motcombe ... 8 E3
Motherwell ... 39 E12
Mottisfont ... 9 E8
Moulton
  Lincs ... 23 C12
  Suff ... 25 J2
  W Nhants ... 22 J7
Mountain Ash ... 7 B9
Mountsorrel ... 22 D4
Mousehole ... 2 J2
Mouswald ... 35 F11
Moy ... 49 E8
Muchalls ... 51 H7
Much Dewchurch ... 14 D3

Much Marcle ... 14 C5
Much Wenlock ... 20 F7
Muir ... 49 K11
Muirdrum ... 51 P4
Muirhead ... 39 D12
Muirkirk ... 39 H12
Muir of Ord ... 48 C6
Muker ... 32 E1
Mulben ... 50 B2
Mullion ... 2 K4
Mullion Cove ... 2 K4
Mundesley ... 24 B7
Mundford ... 24 F3
Munlochy ... 48 C7
Murlaggan ... 47 M10
Murton ... 37 J13
Musbury ... 4 D6
Musselburgh ... 40 F6
Muthill ... 45 H10
Mybster ... 53 C13
Myddle ... 20 D5
Mydroilyn ... 19 Q4
Mynydd Isa ... 26 J3

N
Nafferton ... 33 J12
Nailsea ... 7 D13
Nailsworth ... 14 G7
Nairn ... 49 C9
Nannerch ... 26 H2
Nantwich ... 20 A7
Nappa ... 31 J14
Narberth ... 12 E5
Narborough ... 22 F4
Naseby ... 22 H5
Navenby ... 29 J8
Neap ... 57 G6
Neath ... 13 G11
Necton ... 24 E3
Needham Market ... 25 K5
Needingworth ... 23 H12
Nefyn ... 18 G3
Neilston ... 39 E9
Nelson ... 27 B9
Nenthead ... 36 J6
Neston ... 26 H3
Netheravon ... 8 C6
Netherbury ... 5 D8
Nether Stowey ... 7 H10
Netherthird ... 34 B6
Netherton ... 37 C8
Nethy Bridge ... 49 F11
Netley ... 9 G9
Nettlebed ... 16 G2
Nettleham ... 29 G9
Nettleton ... 29 E10
Nevern ... 12 C4
New Abbey ... 35 G10
New Aberdour ... 50 A7
New Alresford ... 9 D11
Newark-on-Trent .. 28 J7
New Ash Green ... 10 C7
Newbiggin-by-the-
  Sea ... 37 E12
Newbigging ... 40 J3
Newborough ... 18 D4
Newbridge ... 7 B11
Newbridge on Wye .19 Q10
Newbrough ... 36 G7
New Buckenham ... 24 F5
Newburgh
  Aberds ... 50 E8
  Fife ... 40 B5
Newburn ... 37 G10
Newbury ... 15 K13
Newby Bridge ... 31 F9
Newbyth ... 50 B7
Newcastle Emlyn .. 12 C7
Newcastleton ... 36 E3
Newcastle-under-
  Lyme ... 21 B9
Newcastle-upon-
  Tyne ... 37 G11
Newchurch ... 14 A1
New Costessey ... 24 D6
New Cumnock ... 34 B7

New Deer ... 50 C7
Newdigate ... 10 E2
New Earswick ... 33 J8
New Edlington ... 28 E4
Newent ... 14 D6
Newgale ... 12 D2
New Galloway ... 34 F7
Newham ... 10 A5
Newhaven ... 10 J5
New Holland ... 29 B9
Newick ... 10 G5
Newington
  Kent ... 11 C9
  Kent ... 11 F12
Newlot ... 56 E5
New Luce ... 34 G2
Newlyn ... 2 J2
Newmachar ... 50 E7
Newmarket
  Suff ... 25 J1
  W Isles ... 55 D6
Newmill ... 50 B3
New Mills ... 27 G11
Newmilns ... 39 G10
New Milton ... 8 H7
Newnham ... 14 E5
New Pitsligo ... 50 B7
Newport
  Essex ... 17 B10
  IoW ... 9 J10
  Newport ... 7 C12
  Pembs ... 12 C4
  Telford ... 21 D8
Newport-on-Tay ... 40 A7
Newport Pagnell ... 16 A3
Newquay ... 2 E5
New Quay ... 19 Q3
New Radnor ... 20 K3
New Romney ... 11 G11
New Rossington ... 28 E5
New Scone ... 45 G13
Newton ... 31 J13
Newton Abbot ... 4 F2
Newton Arlosh ... 35 H12
Newton Aycliffe ... 32 B4
Newton Ferrers ... 3 G13
Newtongrange ... 40 G6
Newtonhill ... 51 H8
Newton le Willows .. 26 F6
Newton Mearns ... 39 E10
Newtonmore ... 49 J8
Newton Poppleford .. 4 E4
Newton St Cyres ... 4 D2
Newton Stewart ... 34 G5
Newtown
  Hants ... 8 G7
  Hereford ... 14 B5
  Powys ... 20 G2
Newtown St
  Boswells ... 41 K8
New Tredegar ... 7 A10
New Waltham ... 29 D11
Neyland ... 12 F3
Ninfield ... 11 H8
Niton ... 9 K10
Nordelph ... 23 E14
Norham ... 41 J12
Normanby le Wold . 29 E10
Normanton ... 28 B3
Northallerton ... 32 E5
Northam ... 6 J3
Northampton ... 22 J6
North Baddesley ... 9 F8
North Berwick ... 41 E8
North Cerney ... 15 F9
Northchapel ... 9 E14
North Charlton ... 37 A10
North Elmham ... 24 C4
North Ferriby ... 29 B8
North Frodingham . 33 J12
North Hill ... 3 D10
North Hykeham ... 29 H8
Northiam ... 11 G9
North Kessock ... 48 D7
Northleach ... 15 E10
North Molton ... 6 J6
North Newbald ... 29 A8
Northop ... 26 J3

North Petherton......7 H11
Northpunds.........57 K5
North Queensferry...40 E4
Northrepps 24 B7
North Somercotes ..29 E13
North Tawton 3 B14
North Thoresby.....29 E11
North Walsham......24 B7
Northwich 26 H7
North Wingfield 28 H3
Northwold 24 F2
Northwood
IoW 9 H9
London 16 F5
Norton
Glos 14 D7
N Yorks...........33 G9
Suff..............25 J4
Worcs............14 A7
Norton Fitzwarren ...7 J10
Norwich 24 E7
Norwick 57 A7
Nottingham 22 B4
Nuneaton 22 F2
Nunney 8 C2
Nutley 10 G5
Nybster 53 B15

O

Oadby 22 E5
Oakdale 7 B10
Oakengates 21 E8
Oakham 22 E7
Oakley 40 E3
Oban 42 E10
Ochiltree 34 A6
Ockley 10 F2
Odie 56 D6
Odiham 9 C12
Offord D'Arcy 23 J11
Ogbourne St
George 15 J10
Okehampton 3 B13
Old Basing 9 B11
Old Bolingbroke ...29 H12
Oldbury...........14 G5
Old Colwyn 18 C8
Old Deer 50 C6
Old Fletton 23 F10
Oldham...........27 E10
Old Leake 29 K12
Oldmeldrum 50 E7
Old Radnor 14 A1
Olgrinmore 53 C12
Ollaberry 57 D4
Ollerton 28 H5
Olney 22 K7
Ombersley 21 K9
Onchan 30 H3
Onich 44 C2
Opinan 46 B8
Ordhead 50 F5
Ordie 50 G3
Orford 25 K9
Orleton 20 K6
Ormesby St
Margaret 24 D9
Ormiston 40 G7
Ormskirk 26 D5
Orpington 10 C5
Orton 31 D12
Osbournby 23 B9
Oskamull 42 D6
Osmotherley 32 E6
Ossett 27 D13
Oswaldtwistle 27 C8
Oswestry 20 D3
Otford 10 D6
Othery 7 H12
Otley 32 K3
Otterburn 36 D7
Otter Ferry 38 B4
Otterton 4 E4
Ottery St Mary 4 D4
Oulton 24 F10
Oulton Broad......24 F10
Oundle 23 G9

Ousdale 53 G12
Outwell 23 E14
Over 23 H12
Overbister 56 B6
Overseal 21 E13
Overstrand.........24 B7
Overton
Hants 9 C10
Wrex 20 B4
Over Wallop........8 D7
Owston Ferry 28 E2
Oxenholme 31 F11
Oxford 15 F14
Oxnam 36 B6
Oxted 10 D4
Oykel Bridge 52 H5

P

Pabail 55 D7
Paddock Wood 10 E7
Padiham 27 B9
Padstow 2 D7
Paibeil 54 C4
Paignton 4 H2
Pailton 22 G3
Painscastle 13 B15
Painshawfield 37 H9
Painswick 14 F7
Paisley 39 D9
Palgrave 24 H6
Palnackie 35 H9
Pangbourne 16 H1
Papworth Everard ..23 J11
Parkeston 25 M7
Parkhurst 9 H9
Parracombe 6 G5
Partney 29 H13
Parton 30 B5
Pateley Bridge 32 H3
Pathhead 40 G7
Patna 34 B5
Patrick Brompton ..32 E4
Patrington 29 E12
Patterdale 31 C9
Paull 29 B10
Paulton 8 B1
Peacehaven 10 J5
Peak Forest 27 H12
Peasedown St John ..8 B2
Peasenhall 25 J8
Peasmarsh 11 G10
Peebles 40 J5
Peel 30 G2
Pegswood 37 E11
Peinchorran 47 H5
Pembrey 12 F8
Pembridge 14 A3
Pembroke 12 F3
Pembroke Dock 12 F3
Pembury 10 F7
Penally 12 G5
Penarth 7 D10
Pencader 12 C8
Pencoed 13 H13
Pendeen 2 H1
Penderyn 13 F13
Pendine 12 F6
Penicuik 40 G5
Penistone 27 E13
Penkridge 21 E10
Penmachno 18 F7
Penmaenmawr 18 C7
Penmon 54 A7
Pennyghael 42 F7
Penpont 35 D9
Penrhyndeudraeth ..18 G6
Penrith 31 A11
Penryn 2 H5
Pensford 8 A1
Penshaw 37 H12
Penshurst 10 E6
Pensilva 3 E10
Pentraeth 18 C5
Pentrefoelas 18 E8
Penybont 20 K2
Penybontfawr 20 D1
Pen-y-gop 18 F9

Penygroes
Carms.............13 E9
Gwyn 18 E4
Penysarn 18 B4
Penzance 2 J2
Perranporth 2 F5
Perranzabuloe 2 G5
Pershore 15 B8
Perth 45 G13
Peterborough 23 F10
Peterchurch 14 C2
Peterculter 50 G7
Peterhead 50 C10
Peterlee 37 J13
Petersfield 9 E12
Petworth 9 E14
Pevensey 10 J7
Pewsey 8 B6
Pickering 33 F9
Piddletrenthide 5 D11
Pidley 23 H12
Pierowall 56 B4
Pilling 31 K10
Pilton 7 H14
Pinchbeck 23 C11
Pinhoe 4 D3
Pinmore Mains 34 D3
Pinwherry 34 E3
Pirbright 9 B14
Pirnmill 38 F3
Pitlochry 45 D11
Pittenweem 41 C8
Plean 39 B13
Plockton 47 H8
Pluckley 11 E10
Plumpton 36 K4
Plymouth 3 F12
Plympton 3 F13
Plymstock 3 F13
Pocklington 33 K10
Polegate 10 J6
Polesworth 21 F13
Polloch 42 B10
Polperro 3 G9
Polruan 3 G9
Polwarth 41 H10
Polzeath 2 D7
Pontardawe 13 F11
Pontardulais 13 F9
Ponteland 37 F10
Ponterwyd 19 M7
Pontesbury 20 F5
Pontrhydfendigaid ..19 P7
Pontrilas 14 D3
Pontyates 13 F8
Pontyberem 13 E8
Pontypool 7 A11
Pontypridd 7 C9
Pool 2 G4
Poole 8 J5
Poolewe 46 D8
Pooley Bridge 31 B10
Porlock 6 G7
Port Appin 44 E1
Port Askaig 43 M6
Portavadie 38 C4
Port Bannatyne ...38 D5
Port Carlisle 35 G13
Port Charlotte 43 N4
Port Ellen 43 P5
Portencross 38 F6
Port Erin 30 J2
Port Eynon 13 H8
Port Glasgow 39 C8
Portgordon 50 A2
Porth 7 B9
Porthcawl 13 J12
Porthleven 2 J4
Porthmadog 18 G5
Port Isaac 2 D7
Portishead 14 J3
Portknockie 50 A3
Portlethen 51 H8
Port Logan 34 J2
Portmahomack 53 K11
Portnacroish 44 E1
Portnahaven 43 N3

Portnalong 47 H3
Port Nan Giuran ...55 D7
Port Nan Long 54 B6
Port Nis 55 A7
Porton 8 D6
Portpatrick 34 H1
Port Ramsay 42 D10
Portreath 2 G4
Portree 46 G4
Port St Mary 30 J2
Portskerra 53 B10
Portslade-by-Sea ..10 J3
Portsmouth 9 H11
Portsoy 50 A4
Port Talbot 13 H11
Port William 34 J4
Postbridge 3 D14
Potter Heigham ...24 D9
Potterne 8 B4
Potters Bar 16 E7
Potterspury 16 A2
Potton 16 A7
Poulton-le-Fylde...26 B4
Poundstock 3 B9
Powick 14 A7
Poynton 27 G10
Praa Sands 2 J3
Prees 20 C6
Preesall 31 K9
Presbury 27 H10
Prescot 26 F5
Prestatyn 26 G1
Prestbury 15 D8
Presteigne 20 K4
Preston
Borders 41 H10
Dorset 5 E10
E Yorks 29 A10
Kent 11 C13
Lancs 26 B6
Preston Candover ..9 C11
Prestonpans 40 F6
Prestwich 27 E9
Prestwick 34 A4
Prestwood 16 E3
Princes Risborough .16 E3
Princetown 3 D13
Probus 2 G6
Prudhoe 37 G9
Pucklechurch 14 J5
Puddletown 5 D11
Pudsey 27 B13
Pulborough 10 H1
Pulham Market ...24 G6
Pulham St Mary ...24 G7
Pumpsaint 13 B10
Purfleet 17 H10
Purley 10 C4
London 10 C4
W Berks 16 H1
Purton 15 H9
Puttenham 9 C14
Pwllheli 18 G3
Pyle 13 H12

Q

Quadring 23 B11
Quainton 16 D2
Quedgeley 14 E7
Queenborough 11 B10
Queensbury 27 C12
Queensferry
Edin 40 F4
Flint 26 J4
Quorndon 22 D4

R

Rackenford 4 B2
Rackheath 24 D7
Rackwick 56 G2
Radcliffe 27 E8
Radcliffe-on-Trent .22 B5
Radlett 16 F6
Radley 15 G14

Radstock 8 B1
Radyr 7 C10
Raglan 14 F3
Rainham 11 C9
Rainworth 28 J5
Rampside 31 H8
Ramsbottom 27 D8
Ramsey
Cambs 23 G11
Essex 25 M7
IoM 30 F4
Ramseycleuch 35 B13
Ramsgate 11 C14
Rannoch Station ...44 D6
Rapness 56 B5
Rathen 50 A9
Rattray 45 E13
Raunds 23 H8
Ravenglass 30 E6
Ravenshead 28 J4
Ravenstonedale ...31 D13
Rawcliffe 32 J7
Rawmarsh 28 E3
Rawtenstall 27 C9
Rayleigh 17 F13
Reading 16 H2
Reay 53 B11
Redbourn 16 D6
Redbridge 17 G9
Redcar 33 B8
Red Dial 35 J13
Redditch 21 K11
Redesmouth 36 E7
Redhill 10 E3
Red Houses ....5 Jersey
Redland 56 D3
Redlynch 8 F7
Redmile 22 B7
Redmire 32 E2
Red Point 46 E7
Redruth 2 G4
Reepham 24 C5
Reeth 32 E2
Reigate 10 E3
Reiss 53 C15
Renfrew 39 D10
Rennington 37 B11
Repton 22 C2
Resolven 13 F12
Reston 41 G11
Retford 28 F6
Reydon 24 H10
Rhayader 19 P9
Rhewl 26 J2
Rhiconich 52 C4
Rhiw 18 H2
Rhondda 13 G13
Rhoose 7 E9
Rhoslan 18 F4
Rhosllanerchrugog .20 B3
Rhosneigr 18 C3
Rhos-on-Sea 18 B8
Rhossili 12 H8
Rhostryfan 18 E4
Rhubodach 38 C5
Rhuddlan 18 C10
Rhyd-Ddu 18 E5
Rhyl 18 B10
Rhymney 13 F15
Rhynie 50 E3
Riccall 28 A5
Richmond
London 10 B2
N Yorks 32 D3
Rickmansworth ...16 F5
Ridsdale 37 E8
Rievaulx 32 F7
Rigside 39 G13
Rillington 33 G10
Ringford 34 H7
Ringmer 10 H5
Ringwood 8 G6
Ripley
Derbys 28 J3
N Yorks 32 H4

Ripley *continued*
Sur 10 D1
Ripon 32 G5
Ripponden 27 C11
Risca 7 C11
Rishton 27 B8
Roade 22 K6
Roadhead 36 F4
Roberton 36 B3
Robertsbridge 11 G8
Robin Hood's Bay 33 D11
Rocester 21 C12
Rochdale 27 D9
Roche 2 F7
Rochester
Medway 17 J12
Northumb 36 D7
Rochford 17 G13
Rockcliffe
Cumb 36 G2
Dumfries 35 H9
Rockingham 22 F7
Rogart 53 H9
Rogate 9 E13
Roghadal 55 J2
Rolvenden 11 F9
Romford 17 G10
Romsey 9 E8
Ropsley 23 B9
Rosedale Abbey 33 E9
Rosehall 52 H6
Rosehearty 50 A8
Rosemarket 12 F3
Rosemarkie 49 C8
Roskhill 46 G2
Roslin 40 G5
Rosneath 38 B7
Ross 41 K14
Rossett 26 K4
Ross-On-Wye 14 D5
Rosyth 40 E4
Rothbury 37 C9
Rotherham 28 E3
Rothes 49 D13
Rothesay 38 D5
Rothienorman 50 D6
Rothiesholm 56 D6
Rothwell
N Nhants 22 G7
W Yorks 28 B2
Rottal 51 K2
Rottingdean 10 J4
Rowanburn 36 F3
Rowlands Gill 37 H10
Roxburgh 41 K10
Roxby 29 C8
Royal Leamington Spa 22 J2
Royal Tunbridge Wells 10 F6
Royal Wootton Bassett 15 H9
Roybridge 44 A4
Royston
Herts 17 A8
S Yorks 28 D2
Royton 27 E10
Ruabon 20 B4
Ruan Minor 2 K5
Ruardean 14 E5
Rubery 21 J10
Rudston 33 H12
Rufford 26 D5
Rugby 22 H4
Rugeley 21 E11
Ruislip 16 G6
Rumburgh 24 G8
Rumney 7 D11
Runcorn 26 G6
Rushden 23 J8
Rushwick 14 A7
Ruskington 29 J9
Rutherglen 39 D11
Ruthin 26 K2
Ruthven 49 H8
Ruthwell 35 G11
Ryal 37 F9
Rydal 31 D9
Ryde 9 H10
Rye 11 G10
Ryhall 23 D9
Ryhope 37 H13
Ryton 22 H2

S

Sacriston 37 J11
Saddell 38 G2
Saffron Walden 17 B10
Sageston 12 F4
St Abb's 41 G12
St Agnes 2 G5
St Albans 16 E6
St Andrews 41 B8
St Ann's 35 D11
St Arvans 14 G4
St Asaph 18 C10
St Athan 7 E9
St Aubin 5 Jersey
St Austell 3 F8
St Bees 30 C5
St Blazey 3 F8
St Breward 3 D8
St Briavels 14 F4
St Bride's Major 13 J12
St Buryan 2 J1
St Clears 12 E6
St Columb Major 2 E6
St Columb Minor 2 E6
St Combs 50 A9
St Cyrus 51 L6
St David's 12 D1
St Day 2 G5
St Dennis 2 F7
St Dogmaels 12 B5
St Dominick 3 E11
St Enoder 2 F6
St Erth 2 H3
St Fergus 50 B9
St Fillans 45 G8
St Germans 3 F11
St Harmon 19 N9
St Helens 26 F6
St Helier 5 Jersey
St Issey 2 D7
St Ives
Cambs 23 H12
Corn 2 H3
St John's
IoM 30 G2
Jersey 5 Jersey
St Johns Chapel 31 A14
St John's Town of Dalry 34 E7
St Just 2 H1
St Keverne 2 K5
St Leonards 11 J9
St Levan 2 J1
St Mabyn 3 D8
St Margaret's-at-Cliffe 11 E14
St Margaret's Hope 56 G4
St Martin's 5 Jersey
St Mary Bourne 9 B9
St Mary's 56 F4
St Mary's Bay 11 G11
St Mawes 2 H6
St Mellons 7 D11
St Merryn 2 D6
St Minver 2 D7
St Monance 41 C8
St Neots 23 J10
St Newlyn East 2 F6
St Olaves 24 F9
St Osyth 25 P6
St Ouens 5 Jersey
St Peter Port 4 Guern
St Peter's 5 Jersey
St Sampson 4 Guern
St Stephen 2 F7
St Teath 3 D8
St Tudy 3 D8
Salcombe 4 K1
Sale 27 F8
Salen
Argyll 42 D7
Highland 42 B8
Salford 27 F9
Salford Priors 15 A9
Saline 40 D3
Salisbury 8 E6
Sallachy 52 H7
Saltash 3 F12
Saltburn-by-the-Sea 33 B8
Saltcoats 38 F7
Saltfleet 29 E13
Saltfleetby 29 E13
Saltwood 11 F12
Sampford Courtenay 3 B14
Sanaigmore 43 L4
Sandbach 27 J8
Sandbank 38 C6
Sandgate 11 F13
Sandhead 34 J2
Sandhurst 16 J3
Sandleigh 15 F13
Sandness 57 G2
Sandown 9 J10
Sandringham 24 B1
Sandwich 11 D14
Sandy 16 A6
Sanquhar 35 B8
Sarnau 12 A7
Sarnesfield 14 A2
Sarre 11 C13
Satterthwaite 31 E9
Saundersfoot 12 F5
Sawbridgeworth 17 D9
Sawston 17 A9
Sawtry 23 G10
Saxilby 29 G8
Saxlingham Nethergate 24 F7
Saxmundham 25 J8
Saxthorpe 24 B6
Scalasaig 43 J5
Scalby 33 F12
Scalloway 57 J4
Scalpay 55 H4
Scamblesby 29 G11
Scarborough 33 F12
Scardoy 48 C3
Scarinish 42 D2
Scarning 24 D4
Scole 24 H6
Sconser 47 H5
Scopwick 29 J9
Scorton 32 D4
Scotch Corner 32 D4
Scotter 28 D7
Scourie 52 D3
Scousburgh 57 L4
Scrabster 53 B13
Scremerston 41 J13
Scunthorpe 28 C7
Seaford 10 K5
Seaham 37 J13
Seahouses 41 K15
Seamer 33 F12
Sea Palling 24 C9
Seascale 30 D6
Seaton
Cumb 30 A6
Devon 4 E6
Seaton Delaval 37 F12
Seaview 9 H11
Sebergham 36 J2
Sedbergh 31 E12
Sedgefield 32 A5
Seend 8 B4
Selborne 9 D12
Selby 28 A5
Selkirk 36 A3
Sellafield 30 D6
Selsey 9 H13
Sennen 2 J1
Sennybridge 13 D13
Settle 31 H14
Sevenoaks 10 D6
Seven Sisters 13 F12
Severn Beach 14 H4
Severn Stoke 14 B7
Sgarasta Mhor 55 H2
Sgiogarstaigh 55 A7
Shaftesbury 8 E3
Shalcombe 9 J8
Shaldon 4 F3
Shalford 9 C15
Shanklin 9 J10
Shap 31 C11
Sharnbrook 23 J8
Sharpness 14 F5
Shawbury 20 D6
Shawford 9 E9
Shebbear 3 A12
Sheerness 11 B10
Sheffield 28 F2
Shefford 16 B6
Sheigra 52 B3
Shenfield 17 F11
Shepley 27 D12
Shepshed 22 D3
Shepton Mallet 8 C1
Sherborne 5 B10
Sherborne St John 9 B11
Sherburn 33 G11
Sherburn in Elmet 28 A3
Shere 10 E1
Sherfield English 8 E7
Sherfield on Lodden 9 B11
Sheriff Hutton 33 H8
Sheringham 24 A6
Sherston 14 H7
Shiel Bridge 47 K9
Shieldaig 46 F8
Shifnal 21 F8
Shilbottle 37 C10
Shildon 32 B4
Shillingstone 8 G3
Shillington 16 B6
Shinfield 16 J2
Shipdham 24 E4
Shipley 27 B12
Shipston-on-Stour 15 C11
Shipton under Wychwood 15 E11
Shirebrook 28 H4
Shoeburyness 17 G14
Shoreham-by-Sea 10 J3
Shorwell 9 J9
Shotley Bridge 37 H10
Shotley Gate 25 M7
Shottermill 9 D13
Shottisham 25 L8
Shotts 39 D13
Shrewsbury 20 E5
Shrewton 8 C5
Shrivenham 15 H11
Siabost 55 C4
Sible Hedingham 25 M2
Sibsey 29 J12
Sidbury 4 E5
Sidford 4 E5
Sidlesham 9 H13
Sidmouth 4 E5
Silloth 35 H12
Silsden 32 K2
Silverdale 31 G10
Silverstone 16 A1
Silverton 4 C3
Simonsbath 6 H6
Singleton 9 F13
Sittingbourne 11 C10
Sixpenny Handley 8 F5
Sizewell 25 J9
Skegness 29 H14
Skellingthorpe 29 G8
Skelmersdale 26 E5
Skelmorlie 38 D6
Skelton
Cumb 31 A10
Redcar 33 C8
Skerray 52 B8
Skinburness 35 H12
Skipness 38 E4
Skipsea 33 J13
Skipton 32 J1
Skirlaugh 29 A10
Slaidburn 31 J13
Slaithwaite 27 D11
Slaley 37 H8
Slamannan 39 C13
Sleaford 23 A9
Sledmere 33 H11
Sleights 33 D10
Sligachan 47 H4
Slough 16 H4
Smailholm 41 K9
Smarden 11 E9
Smethwick 21 H11
Smithfield 36 G3
Snainton 33 F11
Snaith 28 B5
Snape 25 K8
Sneaton 33 D10
Snettisham 24 B1
Snodland 17 J12
Soham 23 H14
Solas 54 B5
Solihull 21 H12
Solva 12 D1
Somerby 22 D6
Somercotes 28 J3
Somersham 23 H12
Somerton 7 J13
Sonning 16 H2
Sonning Common 16 H2
Sopley 8 H6
Sorbie 34 J5
Sordale 53 B13
Sorisdale 42 B4
Sorn 39 H10
Sortat 53 B14
Soulby 31 C13
Southam 22 J3
Southampton 9 F9
South Anston 28 F4
South Benfleet 17 G12
Southborough 10 E6
South Brent 3 F14
South Cave 29 A8
South Cerney 15 G9
South Elkington 29 F11
Southend 38 K1
Southend-on-Sea 17 G13
Southery 24 F1
South Harting 9 F12
South Hayling 9 H12
South Kelsey 29 E9
South Kirkby 28 C3
Southminster 17 F14
South Molton 6 J5
South Ockendon 17 G10
South Otterington 32 F5
South Petherton 5 B8
South Petherwin 3 C11
Southport 26 D4
South Shields 37 G12
South Tawton 3 B14
South Walsham 24 D8
Southwark 10 B4
South Warnborough 9 C12
Southwell 28 J5
Southwick 10 J3
Southwold 24 H10
South Woodham Ferrers 17 F13
South Wootton 24 C1
South Zeal 3 B14
Sowerby 32 F6
Sowerby Bridge 27 C11
Spalding 23 C11
Spaldwick 23 H10
Sparkford 5 A10
Spean Bridge 44 A4
Speke 26 G5
Spennymoor 32 A4
Spey Bay 50 A2
Spilsby 29 H13
Spittal 12 D3
Spittal of Glenmuick 51 J1
Spittle of Glenshee 45 B12
Spixworth 24 D7
Spofforth 32 J5
Spott 41 F9
Sproatley 29 A10
Stadhampton 16 F1
Staffin 46 E4
Stafford 21 D10
Staindrop 32 B3

Staines-upon-Thames . . . 16 H5
Stainforth
N Yorks . . . 31 H14
S Yorks . . . 28 C5
Stainton
Lincs . . . 29 G9
Mbro . . . 32 C6
Staintondale . . . 33 E11
Staithes . . . 33 C9
Stalbridge . . . 5 B11
Stalham . . . 24 C8
Stallingborough . . . 29 C10
Stalybridge . . . 27 F10
Stamford . . . 23 E9
Stamford Bridge . . . 33 J9
Stamfordham . . . 37 F9
Standish . . . 26 D6
Standlake . . . 15 F12
Stanford le Hope . . . 17 G12
Stanford on Teme . . . 21 K8
Stanhope . . . 37 K8
Stanley
Durham . . . 37 H11
Perth . . . 45 F13
Stannington . . . 37 E11
Stansted Airport . . . 17 C10
Stansted Mountfitchet . . . 17 C10
Stanton . . . 25 H4
Stanton Harcourt . . . 15 F13
Stanton St John . . . 15 F14
Stanway . . . 15 C9
Stanwix . . . 36 H3
Stapleford . . . 22 B3
Staplehurst . . . 11 E8
Starcross . . . 4 F3
Staunton . . . 14 D6
Staunton on Wye . . . 14 B2
Staveley
Cumb . . . 31 E10
Derbys . . . 28 G3
Staxigoe . . . 53 C15
Staxton . . . 33 G12
Steeple Bumpstead 17 A11
Steeple Claydon . . . 16 C2
Stein . . . 46 F2
Stenhousemuir . . . 39 B13
Stenness . . . 57 E3
Stevenage . . . 16 C7
Stevenston . . . 38 F7
Stewarton . . . 39 F9
Steyning . . . 10 H2
Stibb Cross . . . 6 K3
Stichill . . . 41 K10
Stickford . . . 29 H12
Stickney . . . 29 J12
Stillington . . . 32 H7
Stilton . . . 23 G10
Stirling . . . 39 A12
Stobbs . . . 36 C4
Stobo . . . 40 K4
Stock . . . 17 F12
Stockbridge . . . 9 D8
Stockport . . . 27 F10
Stocksbridge . . . 27 F13
Stockton . . . 22 J3
Stockton-on-Tees . . . 32 B6
Stoer . . . 52 F2
Stoke . . . 11 B9
Stoke Albany . . . 22 G7
Stoke Ferry . . . 24 F2
Stoke Fleming . . . 4 J2
Stoke Gabriel . . . 4 H2
Stoke Mandeville . . . 16 E3
Stokenchurch . . . 16 F2
Stoke-on-Trent . . . 21 B9
Stoke Poges . . . 16 G4
Stoke Prior . . . 21 K10
Stokesley . . . 32 C7
Stone
Bucks . . . 16 D2
Glos . . . 14 G5
Staffs . . . 21 C9
Stonehaven . . . 51 J7
Stonehouse
Glos . . . 14 F7
S Lanark . . . 39 F12
Stoneykirk . . . 34 H2
Stonham Aspal . . . 25 K6
Stony Stratford . . . 16 B3
Stornoway . . . 55 D6
Storrington . . . 10 H1
Stotfold . . . 16 B7
Stourbridge . . . 21 H10
Stourpaine . . . 8 G3
Stourport-on-Severn . . . 21 J9
Stow . . . 40 J7
Stow Bardolph . . . 24 E1
Stowmarket . . . 25 K5
Stow-on-the-Wold 15 D11
Strachan . . . 51 H5
Strachur . . . 44 J2
Stradbroke . . . 25 H7
Straiton . . . 34 C4
Stranraer . . . 34 G1
Stratford St Mary . . . 25 M5
Stratford-upon-Avon . . . 15 A11
Strathan . . . 52 B7
Strathaven . . . 39 F11
Strathblane . . . 39 C10
Strathdon . . . 50 F2
Strathkanaird . . . 52 H3
Strathpeffer . . . 48 C5
Strathy . . . 53 B10
Strathyre . . . 44 H7
Stratmiglo . . . 40 B5
Stratton
Corn . . . 3 A10
Glos . . . 15 F9
Stratton St Margaret . . . 15 H10
Streatley . . . 15 J14
Street . . . 7 H13
Strensall . . . 33 H8
Stretford . . . 27 F9
Stretham . . . 23 H14
Stretton
Rutland . . . 23 D8
Staffs . . . 21 D13
Warr . . . 26 G7
Strichen . . . 50 B8
Stromeferry . . . 47 H8
Stromemore . . . 47 H8
Stromness . . . 56 E2
Stronachlachar . . . 44 H6
Strone . . . 38 B6
Strontian . . . 42 B10
Stroud . . . 14 F7
Struy . . . 48 D4
Stubbington . . . 9 G10
Studland . . . 8 J5
Studley . . . 21 K11
Sturminster Marshall . 8 H4
Sturminster Newton . 5 B11
Sturry . . . 11 D12
Sturton . . . 28 F7
Sudbury
Derbys . . . 21 C12
Suff . . . 25 L3
Sulby . . . 30 F3
Sullom . . . 57 E4
Sully . . . 7 E10
Sumburgh . . . 57 M5
Sunderland . . . 37 H13
Sunk Island . . . 29 C11
Sunninghill . . . 16 J4
Sutterton . . . 23 B11
Sutton
Cambs . . . 23 H13
London . . . 10 C3
Sutton Bridge . . . 23 C13
Sutton Coldfield . . . 21 G12
Sutton Courtenay . . . 15 G14
Sutton-in-Ashfield . . 28 H3
Sutton Lane Ends . . . 27 H10
Sutton-on-Sea . . . 29 F14
Sutton-on-Trent . . . 28 H6
Sutton Scotney . . . 9 D9
Sutton-under-Whitestonecliffe . . . 32 F6
Sutton Valence . . . 11 E9
Swadlincote . . . 21 E13
Swaffham . . . 24 E3
Swalcliffe . . . 15 C12
Swalecliffe . . . 11 C12
Swanage . . . 8 K5
Swanley . . . 10 C6
Swansea . . . 13 G10
Sway . . . 8 H7
Swindon . . . 15 H10
Swinefleet . . . 28 B6
Swineshead . . . 23 A11
Swinton
Borders . . . 41 J11
Grt Manchester . . . 27 E8
S Yorks . . . 28 E3
Symbister . . . 57 F6
Symington . . . 40 K2
Symonds Yat . . . 14 E4
Syresham . . . 16 A1
Syston . . . 22 D5

T

Tadcaster . . . 32 K6
Tadley . . . 9 A11
Tain . . . 53 K9
Talgarth . . . 13 C15
Talladale . . . 46 D9
Talley . . . 13 C10
Talsarnau . . . 18 G6
Talybont . . . 19 M6
Tal-y-llyn . . . 19 K7
Talysarn . . . 18 E4
Tamerton Foliot . . . 3 F12
Tamworth . . . 21 F13
Tangmere . . . 9 G13
Tannadice . . . 51 M3
Tanworth-in-Arden 21 J12
Taobh Tuath . . . 55 J1
Tarbert . . . 38 D3
Tarbert / Aird Asaig Tairbeart . . . 55 G3
Tarbet
Argyll . . . 44 J5
Highland . . . 47 M7
Tarbolton . . . 39 H9
Tarland . . . 50 G3
Tarleton . . . 26 C5
Tarporley . . . 26 J6
Tarrant Hinton . . . 8 G4
Tarskavaig . . . 47 K5
Tarves . . . 50 D7
Tarvin . . . 26 J5
Tattenhall . . . 26 K5
Tattersett . . . 24 B3
Taunton . . . 7 J11
Tavistock . . . 3 D12
Tay Bridge . . . 40 A7
Tayinloan . . . 38 F2
Taynuilt . . . 44 F2
Tayport . . . 40 A7
Teangue . . . 47 L6
Tebay . . . 31 D12
Tedburn St Mary . . . 4 D2
Teesside . . . 32 B6
Teignmouth . . . 4 F3
Telford . . . 20 F7
Temple Combe . . . 5 A11
Temple Ewell . . . 11 E13
Temple Sowerby . . . 31 B12
Templeton . . . 12 E5
Tenbury Wells . . . 20 K7
Tenby . . . 12 G5
Tenterden . . . 11 F9
Terrington . . . 33 G8
Terrington St Clement . . . 23 C14
Tetbury . . . 14 G7
Tetney . . . 29 D12
Tetsworth . . . 16 E1
Teviothead . . . 36 C3
Tewkesbury . . . 15 C8
Teynham . . . 11 C10
Thame . . . 16 E2
Thatcham . . . 15 K14
Thaxted . . . 17 B11
Theale . . . 16 H1
The Barony . . . 56 D2
The Mumbles . . . 13 H10
Thetford . . . 24 G3
Thirsk . . . 32 F6
Thornaby on Tees . . . 32 C6
Thornbury . . . 14 H5
Thorndon . . . 25 J6
Thorne . . . 28 C5
Thorney . . . 23 E11
Thornham . . . 24 A2
Thornhill
Dumfries . . . 35 D9
Stirling . . . 45 J8
Thornthwaite . . . 31 B8
Thornton . . . 26 A4
Thornton-le-Dale . . 33 F10
Thorpe . . . 24 E7
Thorpe-le-Soken . . . 25 N6
Thorverton . . . 4 C3
Thrapston . . . 23 H8
Three Legged Cross . . 8 G5
Threlkeld . . . 31 B9
Threshfield . . . 32 H1
Thrumster . . . 53 D15
Thurcroft . . . 28 F3
Thurlby . . . 23 D10
Thurlestone . . . 3 G14
Thurmaston . . . 22 E5
Thursby . . . 36 H2
Thurso . . . 53 B13
Ticehurst . . . 11 G8
Tickhill . . . 28 E4
Tideswell . . . 27 H12
Tidworth . . . 8 C7
Tighnabruaich . . . 38 C4
Tilbury . . . 17 H11
Tillicoultry . . . 40 D2
Tillingham . . . 17 E15
Tilmanstone . . . 11 E13
Timberscombe . . . 7 G8
Timsbury . . . 8 B1
Tingewick . . . 16 B1
Tingwall . . . 56 D3
Tintagel . . . 3 C8
Tintern Parva . . . 14 F4
Tipton . . . 21 G10
Tiptree . . . 25 P4
Tisbury . . . 8 E4
Titchfield . . . 9 G10
Tiverton . . . 4 B3
Toab . . . 57 L4
Tobermory . . . 42 C6
Toberonochy . . . 43 H9
Tobha Mor . . . 54 F4
Toddington . . . 16 C5
Todmorden . . . 27 C10
Tolastadh bho Thuath . . . 55 C7
Tollesbury . . . 25 Q4
Tolpuddle . . . 5 D11
Tomatin . . . 49 F9
Tomdoun . . . 48 H2
Tomintoul . . . 49 G12
Tomnavoulin . . . 49 F13
Tonbridge . . . 10 E6
Tondu . . . 13 H12
Tong . . . 21 F9
Tongue . . . 52 C7
Tonyrefail . . . 7 C9
Topcliffe . . . 32 G6
Topsham . . . 4 E3
Torbay . . . 4 H3
Torcross . . . 4 J2
Torness . . . 48 F6
Torphins . . . 50 G5
Torpoint . . . 3 F12
Torquay . . . 4 G3
Torridon . . . 46 F9
Torroble . . . 52 H7
Torthorwald . . . 35 E11
Torver . . . 31 E8
Toscaig . . . 47 H7
Totland . . . 9 J8
Totley . . . 28 F2
Totnes . . . 4 H1
Totton . . . 9 F8
Towcester . . . 16 A2
Tower Hamlets . . . 10 A4
Tow Law . . . 37 K10
Town Yetholm . . . 36 A7
Trafford Park . . . 27 F8
Tranent . . . 40 F7
Trawsfynydd . . . 18 G7
Trecastle . . . 13 D12
Tredegar . . . 13 F15
Trefeglwys . . . 19 L9
Trefnant . . . 18 C10
Trefriw . . . 18 D7
Tregaron . . . 19 Q6
Tregony . . . 2 G7
Tregynon . . . 20 G2
Treharris . . . 7 B10
Trelech . . . 12 C6
Tremadog . . . 18 G5
Trenance . . . 2 E6
Trentham . . . 21 B9
Treorchy . . . 13 G13
Tresilian . . . 2 G6
Tretower . . . 13 D15
Treuddyn . . . 26 K3
Trimdon . . . 32 A5
Trimley . . . 25 M7
Tring . . . 16 D4
Trinity . . . 5 Jersey
Troon . . . 39 G8
Troutbeck . . . 31 D10
Trowbridge . . . 8 B3
Trull . . . 7 J11
Trumpan . . . 46 E2
Trumpington . . . 23 K13
Trunch . . . 24 B7
Truro . . . 2 G6
Tuddenham . . . 25 H2
Tudweiliog . . . 18 G2
Tullynessle . . . 50 F4
Tummel Bridge . . . 45 D9
Tunstall . . . 25 K8
Turnberry . . . 34 C3
Turriff . . . 50 B6
Turvey . . . 23 K8
Tutbury . . . 21 D13
Tuxford . . . 28 G6
Twatt . . . 56 D2
Tweedmouth . . . 41 H12
Tweedshaws . . . 35 B11
Tweedsmuir . . . 35 A11
Twenty . . . 23 C10
Twyford
Hants . . . 9 E9
Leics . . . 22 D6
Wokingham . . . 16 H3
Tydd St Giles . . . 23 D13
Tydd St Mary . . . 23 D13
Tylorstown . . . 7 B9
Tyndrum . . . 44 F5
Tynemouth . . . 37 G12
Ty'n-y-groes . . . 18 C7
Tywardreath . . . 3 F8
Tywyn . . . 19 K5

U

Uckfield . . . 10 G5
Uddingston . . . 39 D11
Uffculme . . . 4 B4
Uffington . . . 15 H12
Ufford . . . 25 K8
Ugborough . . . 3 F14
Uig . . . 46 E4
Ulbster . . . 53 D15
Ulceby . . . 29 C9
Ulceby Cross . . . 29 G13
Uley . . . 14 G6
Ullapool . . . 52 J3
Ulsta . . . 57 D5
Ulverston . . . 31 G8
Unapool . . . 52 E4
Upavon . . . 8 B6
Uphill . . . 7 F12
Upper Chapel . . . 13 C14
Upper Heyford . . . 15 D14
Upper Hindhope . . . 36 C6
Upper Poppleton . . . 32 J7
Upper Tean . . . 21 C11
Uppertown . . . 56 G4
Uppingham . . . 22 F7
Upton . . . 26 J5
Upton Snodsbury . . . 15 A8
Upton upon Severn . . 14 B7

Upwey............... 5 E10
Urchfont............. 8 B5
Urmston........... 27 F8
Usk................ 14 F2
Usselby............ 29 E9
Uttoxeter 21 C11
Uyeasound.......... 57 B6

V

Valley 18 C2
Veness............ 56 C5
Ventnor........... 9 K10
Verwood............ 8 G5
Veryan............. 2 H7
Vickerstown....... 30 H7
Vidlin............. 57 F5
Virginia Water..... 16 J5
Voe................ 57 F5
Voy................ 56 E2

W

Waddesdon 16 D2
Waddingham....... 29 E8
Waddington........ 29 H8
Wadebridge......... 2 D7
Wadhurst 10 F7
Wainfleet All
   Saints.......... 29 H13
Wakefield 28 B2
Walberswick 25 H9
Walcott........... 29 J10
Walderslade 17 J12
Waldron........... 10 H6
Walford 20 J4
Walkerburn 40 K6
Walkeringham 28 E6
Wallasey.......... 26 F4
Wallingford 16 G1
Walls............. 57 H3
Wallsend 37 G12
Walmer........... 11 E14
Walpole 23 D13
Walsall 21 G11
Walsham le Willows .25 H4
Walsoken 23 D13
Waltham........... 29 D11
Waltham Abbey 17 F8
Waltham Forest ... 17 G8
Waltham on the
   Wolds.......... 22 C7
Walton-on-Thames .10 C2
Walton-on-the-
   Naze........... 25 N7
Wanborough 15 H11
Wandsworth 10 B3
Wangford.......... 24 H9
Wansford 23 F9
Wantage.......... 15 H13
Warboys.......... 23 G12
Wardington 15 B13
Wardle 26 K7
Ware.............. 17 D8
Wareham 8 J4
Wargrave 16 H2
Wark............. 36 F7
Warkworth....... 37 C11
Warley........... 21 H11
Warminster 8 C3
Warrington 26 G7
Warton 31 G10
Warwick 22 J1
Wasbister........ 56 C3
Washaway 3 E8
Washford 7 H9
Washingborough ...29 G9
Washington
   T&W........... 37 H12
   W Sus..........10 H2

Watchet 7 G9
Watchfield 15 G11
Waterbeach 23 J13
Waterhead 51 K3
Waterhouses 21 A11
Wateringbury 10 D7
Waterlooville....... 9 G11
Watford 16 F6
Wath upon Dearne .. 28 E3
Watlington
   Norf 24 D1
   Oxon............16 F1
Watten 53 C14
Watton 24 E4
Waunfawr 18 E5
Weachyburn 50 B5
Wearhead.......... 36 K7
Weasenham 24 C3
Weaverham 26 H7
Weaverthorpe 33 G11
Wedmore 7 G13
Wednesbury 21 G10
Wednesfield 21 F10
Weedon Bec 22 J5
Weeley 25 N6
Welburn 29 J8
Weldon
   N Nhants 23 G8
   Northumb......37 D10
Welford
   W Berks 15 J13
   W Nhants 22 G5
Wellesbourne 15 A11
Wellingborough ... 22 J7
Wellington
   Som 4 B5
   Telford 20 E7
Wells............. 7 G14
Wells-next-the-Sea .24 A4
Welney 23 F14
Welshampton 20 C5
Welshpool 20 F3
Welton 29 G9
Welwyn Garden City .16 D7
Wem 20 D6
Wembury 3 G13
Wemyss Bay 38 C6
Wendover.......... 16 E3
Wensley 32 E3
Wenvoe............ 7 D10
Weobley 14 A3
Werrington 3 C11
West Bergholt 25 N4
Westbourne........ 9 G12
West Bridgford ... 22 B4
West Bromwich ... 21 G11
West Burton 32 F2
Westbury
   Shrops 20 F4
   Wilts............ 8 C3
Westbury-on-
   Severn.......... 14 E6
Westbury-sub-
   Mendip.......... 7 G14
West Calder........40 G3
West Coker 5 B9
Westcott 10 E2
West Dean 8 E7
West End 9 F9
Westerham 10 D5
West Felton 20 D4
Westfield 11 H9
West Grinstead ... 10 G2
West Haddon 22 H5
Westhill 50 G7
Westhoughton 26 E7
West Kilbride 38 F7
West Kingsdown ... 10 C6
West Kirby 26 G3
Westleton 25 J9
West Linton 40 H4
West Looe 3 F10
West Lulworth 8 K3
West Malling 10 D7
West Meon 9 E11
West Mersea 25 P5

Westminster 10 A4
West Moors......... 8 G5
Weston 21 D10
Weston-super-Mare .7 E12
Westonzoyland 7 H12
West Rasen 29 F9
Westruther......... 41 H9
West Thorney 9 G12
West Wellow 9 F8
West Woodburn 36 E7
Wetheral........... 36 H3
Wetherby 32 K6
Wetwang 33 J11
Weybourne 24 A6
Weybridge 16 J5
Weyhill 9 C8
Weymouth 5 F10
Whaley Bridge 27 G11
Whalley........... 27 B8
Whalton 37 E10
Whatton 22 B6
Whauphill 34 J5
Whaw 32 D1
Wheathampstead...16 D6
Wheatley
   Notts 28 F6
   Oxon...........15 F14
Wheatley Hill......37 K12
Wheaton Aston..... 21 E9
Wheldrake 33 K8
Whicham 30 F7
Whickham 37 G11
Whimple........... 4 D4
Whipsnade........ 16 D5
Whissendine 22 D7
Whitburn 40 G2
Whitby 33 C10
Whitchurch
   Bristol 14 K5
   Bucks...........16 D3
   Devon........... 3 D12
   Hants 9 C9
   Hereford 14 E4
   Shrops 20 B6
White Bridge......48 G5
Whitehall Village ...56 D6
Whitehaven 30 C5
Whitehouse........ 38 D3
Whitekirk 41 E9
Whiteparish 8 E7
Whitfield 11 E14
Whithorn 34 K5
Whitland 12 E5
Whitley Bay 37 F12
Whitonditch 15 J11
Whitsome......... 41 H11
Whitstable 11 C12
Whitstone 3 B10
Whittington
   Derbys 28 G2
   Lancs 31 G12
   Shrops 20 C4
   Staffs 21 F12
Whittlebury 16 A1
Whittlesey 23 F11
Whittlesford 17 A9
Whitwell
   Derbys 28 G4
   IoW 9 K10
Whitwick 22 D3
Whitworth 27 D9
Whixley........... 32 J6
Whome............ 56 G3
Wick
   Hants 8 F6
   Highland........53 D15
   V Glam 13 J13
Wicken 23 H14
Wickford 17 F12
Wickham 9 G10
Wickham Market ...25 K8
Wickwar........... 14 H6
Widdrington 37 D11
Widecombe in the
   Moor........... 4 F1

Widemouth Bay 3 A9
Wide Open........ 37 F11
Widnes 26 G6
Wigan 26 E6
Wigmore
   Hereford 20 K5
   Medway 11 C9
Wigston 22 F5
Wigton 35 J13
Wigtown.......... 34 H5
Wilkhaven 53 K11
Willand 4 C4
Willaston 26 H4
Willenhall........ 21 F10
Willersley 14 B2
Willesborough 11 E11
Willingdon......... 10 J7
Willington
   Bedford 16 A6
   Durham 37 K10
Williton 7 H9
Willoughby 29 G13
Wilmington 4 D6
Wilmslow......... 27 G9
Wilnecote 21 F13
Wilton............. 8 D6
Wimblington 23 F13
Wimborne Minster .. 8 F5
Wincanton 5 A11
Winchcombe...... 15 D9
Winchelsea....... 11 H10
Winchester 9 E9
Windermere 31 E10
Windsor 16 H4
Windygates 40 C6
Wing 16 D3
Wingate 37 K13
Wingham 11 D13
Winkleigh 3 A14
Winscombe 7 F13
Winsford 26 J7
Winslow 16 C2
Winster 27 J13
Winston 32 C3
Winterborne
   Stickland........ 8 G3
Winterbourne Abbas .5 E10
Winterton
   N Lincs 29 C8
   Norf 24 C9
Wirksworth 28 J1
Wisbech 23 D13
Wisbech St Mary .. 23 E13
Wisborough Green .10 G1
Wishaw........... 39 E13
Witchampton 8 G4
Witchford 23 H14
Witham 17 D13
Witheridge 4 B1
Withern 29 F13
Withernsea 29 B12
Withington 15 E9
Witley 9 D14
Witnesham 25 K6
Witney 15 E12
Wittersham 11 G10
Wiveliscombe 7 J9
Wivelsfield....... 10 G4
Wivenhoe 25 N5
Wix.............. 25 N5
Woburn 16 B4
Woburn Sands ... 16 B4
Woking 16 K5
Wokingham 16 J3
Wolf's Castle..... 12 D3
Wollaston 23 J8
Wolsingham 37 K9
Wolverhampton ...21 G10
Wolverton 16 B3
Wolviston........ 32 B6
Wombwell....... 28 D3
Wonersh........ 10 E1
Wonston 9 D9
Woodbridge 25 L7
Woodbury 4 D5
Woodchester....... 14 F7

Woodchurch 11 F10
Woodcote 16 G1
Woodgreen......... 8 F6
Woodhall Spa 29 H13
Woodhouse....... 28 F3
Woodhouse Eaves .. 22 D4
Woodley.......... 16 H2
Woodstock 15 E13
Woofferton 20 K6
Wookey........... 7 G14
Wookey Hole....... 7 G14
Wool 8 J3
Woolacombe 6 G3
Woolavington 7 G12
Wooler 37 A8
Woolwich 10 B5
Woolwich Ferry ... 10 B5
Wooperton 37 A9
Woore 21 B8
Wootton Bridge ... 9 H10
Wootton Wawen ... 21 K12
Worcester 14 A7
Worfield 21 G8
Workington 30 B5
Worksop 28 G4
Wormit 40 A6
Worsbrough 28 D3
Wortham 24 H5
Worthing 10 J2
Wotton under Edge .14 G6
Wragby 29 G10
Wrangle 29 J13
Wrea Green 26 B4
Wrentham 24 G9
Wretham 24 G4
Wrexham 20 A4
Writtle 17 E11
Wroughton 15 J10
Wroxham 24 D7
Wroxton 15 B13
Wyberton 23 A11
Wye 11 E11
Wylye 8 D5
Wymondham
   Leics 22 D7
   Norf 24 E6

Y

Yalding 11 E8
Yarcombe 4 C6
Yardley Hastings .. 22 K7
Yarm 32 C6
Yarmouth 9 J8
Yarnton.......... 15 E13
Yarrow 36 A2
Yate 14 H6
Yatton 7 E13
Yaxley 23 F10
Yeadon 27 A12
Yealmpton 3 F13
Yelverton 3 E13
Yeovil 5 B9
Yetminster 5 C9
Y Felinheli 18 D5
York 32 J1
Youlgreave....... 27 J13
Yoxall 21 E12
Yoxford 25 J9
Ysbyty Ifan...... 18 F8
Ysbyty Ystwyth ... 19 N7
Ystalyfera........ 13 F11
Ystradgynlais 13 E11

Z

Zennor 2 H2